# A Quest of Faith
# in
# the Darkness

Brandi "Avi Queen" Watts

# A Quest of Faith in the Darkness

# A Quest of Faith in the Darkness

*Written and experienced By Author Brandi "Avi Queen" Watts*

    The Most High does indeed work in mysterious ways, such as those you are about to read. With this notebook, I was instructed to record the proof and return of The Most High Ahayah's wonders and blessings. Consider this a reminder that "Miracles do still happen in the modern-day". Everything in this book you are about to read is true although filtered for audiences of most ages. Also, for the sake of copyright and compliance; Most of the characters will be addressed with substitute names. Be prepared to read about the woes and failures in this quest as well as the blessings and revelations. I know you all have heard this before but "you have to take the bad with the good". Every quest is different from the other and every awakening happens in a personally customized way. Oh snap! I believe I have said too much. Read it for yourself and see what I mean.

*"Write down the vision and make it plain upon tables; that He may run that readeth " -Habakkuk 2:2*

*For God(Ahayah) so loved the world that He gave his only begotten son(YaShaya), that whosoever believeth in Him may not perish; But have everlasting life.*
-John 3:16

## Table of Contents

Chapter 1: The Storm of the Century
Chapter 2: Covered or Filled?
Chapter 3: The Things for which We Pray
Chapter 4: The Unimaginable
Chapter 5: Ashah Chayil
Chapter 6: Under The Tree
Chapter 7: Wisdom the Beloved
Chapter 8: Walk By Faith
Chapter 9: Things Unseen
Chapter 10: Still Standing
Chapter 11: Grapes in the Wilderness
Chapter 12: No Weapon Formed
Chapter 13: The Power of Fasting
Chapter 14: The BullFrog
Chapter 15: Picture This
Chapter 16: As In the Days of Noah
Chapter 17: Positioned
Chapter 18: The Greatest Love Story

# A Reminder of Grace...

*Blessed are the poor in spirit, For theirs is the Kingdom of Heaven.(Matt 5:3)*
*Blessed are those who mourn, For they will be comforted(Matt 5:4)*
*Blessed are the meek, For they will inherit the earth.(Matt 5:5)*
*Blessed are they who hunger after righteousness; for they will be filled.(Matt 5:6)*
*Blessed are the merciful, For they will be shown mercy.(Matt 5:7)*
*Blessed are the pure in heart, For they will see Ahayah.(Matt 5:8)*
*Blessed are the peacemakers, For they will be called the children of Ahayah. (Matt 5:9)*
*Blessed are those persecuted in righteousness; For theirs is the kingdom of Heaven.(Matt 5:10)*
*Blessed are ye when men shall revile you, and persecute you, and shall say all manner of evil against you falsely; for my sake. (Matt 5:11) Blessed are they who hear the word of The Most High and keep it.(Luke 11:28)*

## Interlude by Remembrance

In November of 2020, I lost my baby brother Trey to a tragic motorcycle accident. That's when things began to fall completely apart for me. This was all leading up to something unfathomable. Imagine my reaction to hearing that my only baby brother, whom I promised I'd always come back for; was gone. The pain almost consumed me. I remember lashing out on people who only wanted to help, lashing out on people who didn't seem to care and those that cared but didn't know what to say. Truth is, I had come to the conclusion that it wouldn't matter what anyone said because Trey was gone and their words wouldn't bring him back.

Now If you're starting to think that this will be one of those "Lazarus situations", You're right and wrong. Wrong because my brother isn't rising from where he lies and right because the name Lazarus in the Bible actually means "God has helped". So if you haven't figured it out by now; We are about to go on a quest. For me it's deja vu but, for you it will be a spark that hopefully lights your path to begin your own "Quest of Faith in the Darkness". I dedicate this work to My Heavenly Father, Ahayah, His Holy Spirit(The Rawach Qadash) and His son YaShaya Hamashiach. I pray that He may be pleased with my faith, obedience, and determination.

I dedicate this book in loving memory of my brother "Trey Watts", my Grandmother, "Gloria Van", and my cousin, "Lakestra Turner". To all of my brothers(Ahchyam) &sisters(Ahchwath) aka my people of The Lost Tribes of Israel. I pray you all be found and begin to seek THE TRUTH as I did and am still. Shalawam and let's begin!

# Chapter 1

# The Storm of the Century

    Newsflashes were popping up everywhere, concerning the snow that was soon to come. This was being described as the modern day "Storm of the Century!" People were already in terror of the Covid Pandemic spreading and now came a snowstorm that would surely reconstruct what was normal and enforce the temporary laws of social distancing. Everyone everywhere was in a severe panic. People were going out and buying all of the toilet paper, Clorox wipes, and bleach. I remember seeing empty shelves that once held hundreds of bottles of hand sanitizer, in almost every store. Food was scarce in smaller cities and people were stocking up on what they could find.

  Growing up in Dallas, Texas; Snow was almost a fairytale for us. We knew heat, rain, and even the occasional hail. But, this was something we knew not. I know many of you are thinking "She's tripping, It wasn't that bad!" You're wrong! It was that bad. Bad enough to have stores close down, jobs canceled, and people longing for the churches to reopen.

  Before, I go completely into the "Storm of the Century", let me take you back to the month prior. It was January, two months after Trey's passing and one month before my "Awakening." I remember waking up from an uncomfortable restless night of sleeping in my car at 6:35 a.m. The sun hadn't risen yet, but something amazing was about to transpire. I awakened and immediately checked the time via my phone. "6:35 again" I thought to myself.

This was the third day this week. "Maybe I am overthinking this," I said. It had only been a few days since I'd given up drugs permanently and for some reason which I'll never know The Most High had decided to dub me redeemed and forgiven. After years of struggling on and off with this drug, I was finally set free. YaShaya heard my sincere and humble cries on that cold, stormy night. However, getting back to the morning that changed my life forever; I decided to check my email and stumbled across an email sent as a notification from an app called "Abide". When I opened it John 6:35 stuck out like a sore thumb. Abide was an app that conveniently quoted scriptures and gave vividly specific scenarios that would cause anyone to instantly fall into self-evaluation. While listening, I had an epiphany. Suddenly I was overcome with conviction and repentance of all the things I had done in the past. I even felt convicted of things that I was doing the day before. On that day, the light came to dwell within me indefinitely. I began to search for scriptures, almost as if being led to one in particular. "Found it!" I said out loud, remembering that I was in the car alone.

I began to shed tears while reading Acts 19:19. Was this a message? Was Ahayah whom I once rebelled against now speaking to me? "Why me?" I asked while still crying. Realizing this was truly confirmation and an opportunity for redemption, I gathered all of my crystals and chunked them out of the window. Now, At this point; The sun had begun to rise, people were up and moving about; leaving for work. I didn't care. I continued to read and then began to search for my misleading books of numerology and craft. I grabbed them, burned them, and drove off. Many people pray for these types of miracles and signs. There I was, a young sinner now forgiven and being redeemed from 24 years of lies, rebellion and dysfunction. It didn't mean I was suddenly perfect or flawless. It meant that I had been given help and that guidance was sure to accompany me.

Back to the following month, which was February; The snow was moving in on us and my phone had been acting so weird. On a Wednesday, Stylez had to work and It was arranged for me to stay at his coworker Skreet's hotel room. I remember thinking, "Well since my phone isn't working, I can at least watch a movie." YaShaya had plans to water that seed, which was planted many years ago by my grandmother, Gloria. I proceeded to watch a movie called "How to Build a Girl." It was the story of a girl named Johanna, who was given an opportunity to fulfill her dreams prematurely. She was an aspiring music journalist, thrust into a life which she was not yet ready for. Although we had different dreams, this surely resonated with me. She was tricked into wanting to be like those who deemed her unworthy. This angered me. Who are they to pick and choose who is to be considered "worthy?" None of us are worthy lest we find His grace and mercy. I was zoned out and tuned in for two hours. In conclusion, Johanna found her purpose and her rightful place. However, due to coveting desires she first had to experience the pain, the torment, the feeling of lowness, and depression; These were the building blocks for her to become that person which she was created to be. Resonating with anyone yet? This movie is definitely a "must watch." Look at me sounding like an experienced movie critic.

The point is that most people would rather find a shortcut to success; Rather than to work hard and suffer long for it. I went both routes for several years and now I have realized the truth is "You can not serve two masters." All of my life, despite the distractions and problems from which I suffered, I have sang and written music. Although I grew up in the church, I was still determined to be the next "Big R&B Queen". I put in the work and the practice. My mom even made investments, sacrificed financially, and time-wise but getting pregnant at fifteen seemed to have destroyed the whole plan. When I was fifteen, I made many mistakes. One of them was wanting to fit in. Obviously, I was in a hurry to grow up. I wound up getting pregnant unknowingly and aborted the baby five months later. I remember it like it was yesterday. I didn't want to but I understood what me being a teen mom made my mom feel. She wasn't a failure and this wasn't her fault. The strange thing about it all was that even before I knew that I was pregnant, it was revealed by the holy spirit through my grandmother, Gloria. Basically, what's done in the dark always comes to the light. Ahayah still had a plan for me even though I'd fornicated, lied, and murdered. Ahayah had a plan for David and Saul so how insane is it that he has one for me? Don't you know that Ahayah has a plan for you and He has given it unto YaShaya's hand to help you get there? First, He has to break you gracefully so that He can put you back together in a stronger, wiser, and better form. He is still in the business of making old things new! The master builder and greatest architect wants to make a masterpiece out of your brokenness. Isn't it Interesting that Johanna comes from the Hebrew name Yachannah and it means "God has graced or favored." So understand that if this book has found you, Grace has been extended to you as it was to me.

    After watching the movie, I began to pray and sing in worship. Then, shortly after i fell asleep. When I awoke, I began to wonder if my phone's weirdness was an act of Ahayah. I decided to test my newfound faith. I turned, looked at my phone, and commanded it to turn on. I know you might be laughing, but I did. It didn't come on though. I just knew it would soon. So, I commanded a few more times. Eventually, I stopped trying; Not because I was giving up, but because it was not time for it to turn on yet. Perhaps, The Most High had more for me to take from this lesson. This meant it would take more time than I could imagine. When Stylez and Skreet returned, It was time to go. Honestly, I was homeless at this time. We would either sleep in the car, hustle for a hotel room, or go over to one of Stylez' homeboy's houses. Two out of three of these options were dangerous and yet, Our Heavenly Father never ceased to protect us. I know Christ was there with me through it all because, once while staying over one of Stylez' associates Greg's house; We encountered many strange supernatural incidents. We met a witch who was in the process of casting a spell on Stylez' friend Dre; which resulted in us praying for him to come out of a dark state of mind. Shortly afterwards we encountered a spirit lurking in the bathroom and mysteriously there was candle wax poured into the sink each morning. We will get into the full explanation of those at another time. However, Ahayah led us to Fort Worth on this specific evening after Stylez got paid. Unsuspectingly, we were led to be laid away and put up.

    Almost as soon as we got there, the snow began to fall harder and finally, the "Storm of the Century" had commenced. Now, mind you this was the week leading up to my 29th birthday which soon we would refer to as my time of awakening. We were being fed all kinds of delicious home-cooked meals by Stylez' dad and watching all kinds of interesting movies as a family. Yet, it wouldn't be long before the tests, trials and revelations came upon us.

So although we were snowed in, We most definitely weren't stuck. No, we were actually right where we were supposed to be at that time. Let me remind you of one of the most important principles to understanding my story. That principle is that "THERE ARE NO COINCIDENCES!" No, there are NONE! Not even one. Understand that when Ahayah gives the plan to YaShaya, there will be no limits to what He will do to get your attention and put that plan into action. He will arrange the timing, He will send the people, He will line up the events, He will even paint you signs along the way to encourage you to take the necessary steps towards achieving those plans. So during this week of being snowed in, Every morning I was led to go outside at 6:35 am and sit in the car for prayer, my daily abide, praise and worship. It's amazing how these 2-3 minute devotions became 2-3 hour prayers.

Everything I was asking, YaShaya was beginning to reveal right before my eyes. A few times Stylez came out to check on me and ended up joining in praise or prayer. He liked when I did those older Baptist church hymns. It was uplifting and insightful. Some days the snow would knock out the electricity and we would light candles or charge our phones in the car for light in the house. On other days the hot water would be frozen and we'd take cold baths. We quickly learned how the Eskimos felt. Well, not exactly but we learned a new level of adapting. Some days I would get to talk to my babies on Duo who were living with relatives for the last 3 years. Even that will be addressed in the next book "Such A Time as This". Mostly, I was seeking though. It seems like seeking the truth became an addiction. It was to the point where I constantly needed more.

Finally, the day I had been waiting for came. February 18, 2021. This day was a blessing in itself. It was truly a blessing to experience 29 years. Even more, it was a blessing to share it with Stylez. On that day, I prayed a powerful 21- minute deliverance prayer and I believe that through YaShaya the power to break myself, with the agreement of my Grandmother Melinya; from our family's generational curse; was given. Ahayah was showing me the power of Christ in ways I never knew were possible. I remember walking back into the house and waiting for Stylez to pop out. He had somehow found time to sneak off and get me a gift in this treacherous weather. I thought for sure that I'd be taking a rain check on gifts this year. However, to my surprise, there were two gift bags laid out on the couch. One contained a beautifully written love letter which caused me to shed tears along with a purple butterfly-decorated notebook. The other was a new large silver purse. I was so grateful and filled with joy, but there was so much more on the way and this was only the beginning. The very next day I received two phone calls. The first was a dinner invite from my mom and little sisters. Teece and LuLu are their names. I was elated and excited! We were going for sushi in downtown Fort Worth. This was before I'd learned that we should only eat fish that has scales. This was commanded of us in the book of Leviticus. The second call was from my grandmother.

She told me she had a surprise for me and to call her after dinner. Ahayah had once again given plans to YaShaya with my name in them and the Holy Spirit was guiding me right to a victory like none I had ever seen in my life. I enjoyed my sushi and fellowship with my Mom and sisters. I get to act so silly around them without feeling judged. They're all silly also; when it's just us. When dinner was over I hurried to call my granny back. She told me that someone wanted to talk to me , but they had to leave and would be back. I had been praying all these prayers and now they were all being answered. One of my biggest prayers was for my biological dad to surrender unto Christ and be released from prison. Later that evening we had to head back to Dallas to prepare for my big birthday concert. This show was the talk of the town and everyone was coming out. This was going to be the night I brought out and introduced every artist I had been working with for the last year. The show was titled "A Night to Remember With Avi Queen and Friends." People were talking about it everywhere for weeks and after surviving the "Storm of the Century" we thought it would be perfect.

Clearly, Ahayah had different plans because moments before showtime i received a call with the news that a pipe had burst at my friend Net's mom's club. You know what that means? No show! I wasn't angry though. I initially suspected this to be a spiritual or demonic attack; but then I came to the realization that "Everything happens for a reason." The good thing is that no one was hurt. All things would be revealed in due time.

The next day I got another call. This call brought me great joy. My Dad was home from prison and would be at my step mom's house later that evening.

I couldn't wait to pull up. It had been years since he was incarcerated. When it was time, Stylez And I pulled up. The gift of joy overtook my whole body. This was not only a blessing, but proof that miracles do happen in the modern day! Seeing my dad after all those years brought me tears of joy. I hoped and believed that He would remain free this time. I played for him the song that I'd recorded to express the way It felt to lose Trey and watched everyone in the room break down in remembrance of my baby brother. To some this would be sad, but for us at that moment we remembered Trey. We continued celebrating my dad's freedom and then it was time to go so that He could make it to the halfway house by curfew. For him this was a chance at redemption and for me this was a new beginning; a form of victory.

## Chapter 2

## Covered or Filled

Over the next few days, The Rawach began to reveal and teach things to me. I learned the truth about the Sabbath and so much more. I cried so many tears during that time. I couldn't understand "Why me?" Why would Christ choose me to save, teach, and transform? I knew that I wasn't worthy and yet He continued to show me mercy and grace. I began to receive words and messages as if I were to evangelize or at least share them. In today's society, If someone were to encounter YaShaya; chances are they wouldn't even pay enough attention to realize who it is. It's sad to say, but once they'd realized whom it was standing before them; Even then they would probably ask for a granted wish as if He were some sort of genie. Me, If I encountered Christ I would ask to become as wise as Solomon. I've already been blessed to experience moments that required Moses' dedication, Daniel's faith, and Saul's transformation. Ahayah's grace is way more than enough for me though. So I began to see confirmations everywhere I turned and soon all I desired was to be pleasing in His eyes. The Most High began to speak to me through anything that caught my attention. I would filter messages down to the original Hebrew or Greek root words according to Strong's Concordance. This was a way to understand things as they were intended to be understood.

The Rawach Qadash began to speak directions, instructions, comforting words, ideas, and even things that made me laugh. A strong, confident faith was born in me and I grew to love every moment of it, even the trying times. I became determined to live up to as many of Ahayah's expectations as possible. Though I still couldn't be perfect or anywhere near it; He would always find a way to let me know that He loves me and forgives me. I began to be alone a lot during this time. I felt that most of the people who knew me as D'va wouldn't understand. Once everything had taken place and the pieces were being placed back together, it was in such a profound way. I was being made new and getting ready to walk into a new season. I believe that it is safe to say that whenever any of my friends decided to call they would get an ear full of testimony and newfound wisdom. I have to stop and say "All Praise be to Ahayah The Most High, YaShaya Hamashiach and the Rawach Qadash!" It is an honor of which I am so undeserving to be able to feel this close to my creator. I admit at first, I was a little nervous; But how great is it to realize that He'd planned "My Return" before I was even lost? If you're reading this story, understand that He has planned yours too. Even in the midst of my storms, I will hold on with strong faith and not let it waiver. It will surely continue to grow. I am proud to say that I am now willingly a servant of The Almighty. One day YaShaya provided Stylez and I with free food on Ledbetter Rd. This was so significant because it was literally an answer to my prayers and thoughts from only moments before it happened. I remember being so hungry and not eating all morning. We didn't have a lot of money that day and what we had we'd put into gas. Just as we passed the street that Trey once lived on, I looked up and saw the number 1111 on a church building we were driving towards. Of Course now I understand that seeing those numbers in a certain sequence has nothing to do with Abba; but back then I didn't know yet. A few moments later, We were flagged down by a man with a sign. He directed us to free food that would last a week or two if we were resourceful with it. More praises went up from my heart unto My father. I can't even begin to imagine what Ahayah is setting up next, but I know it will be a full-proof plan. I know it will be unlike any of those half-baked plans that I used to continuously concoct for myself. They always went horribly wrong. Usually, they were led by my own understanding and that's a recipe for disaster every time. Ahayah has begun to grant me wisdom and YaShaya consistently lights the way. Every fortress or barrier has been broken down and crushed right before my eyes. Blessings have started falling into my grasp from every direction. Questions and answers flow dramatically like the waters of the rushing sea. Discernment is becoming stronger and now being a tool in defense to protect my heart and mind. Surely, Christ is alive and well!

When the next rising came, Stylez and I awoke excited for what we thought would happen that day. We had gone back to his parent's home. Yet, everything went totally opposite. A conversation took place between us and them which led us to turn away. YaShaya made it clear eventually and showed me that this "Had to Happen." The pressures of feeling abandoned had to eat away at us. Remember Romans 8:28 "All Things Work Together for the Good of Those who Love The Most High." We were beginning to believe the lies and finally, the pain and deceit of the world had to separate us. Oh, but we'd soon see blessings!

Soon, the gematria was revealed to me and the dark deceit embedded in most who have been using it for many years and the many false doctrines weaved into it as well. These exposed truths led me to more understanding of the world and what was really surrounding me. I knew I was safe though. I was beginning to wonder if this was what it means to be filled with the Spirit. Is it better to be filled or to be covered? To me Being covered is more like having liability insurance. They've got you covered to a certain extent. However, being filled is that Premium insurance policy. It is 360 all around and inside. You know you are good before the damage, when it's happening, and they're going to provide a rental until the damage is fixed. How amazing is that?! I love the feeling of knowing that Christ is constant and reassuring; The Rawach gives comfort even in the worst times and that too is beautiful. What do you do other than stand in awe when The Almighty purposely makes known to you His promises?

"And I will cleanse them from all of their iniquity, whereby they have sinned against me; and I will pardon all of their iniquities, whereby they have transgressed against. And it shall be to me, a name of joy. A praise and an honor before all of the nations of the earth. Which shall hear all the good that I do unto them; And they shall fear and tremble for all the goodness and for all the prosperity that I procure unto it." -Jeremiah 33:8-9

Grand Rising Abba Ahayah,

   Thank you for waking me, my family and my loved ones on this beautiful day, which was not promised. Father, thank you for all of these beautiful revelations over a short time. Thank you for choosing to love and protect me. I ask that you continue to keep me and allow Your Spirit to continuously dwell within me. For it is better to be filled! Forgive me for my transgressions against you, myself and my brothers & sisters. Cleanse me from Head to toe! Wash me in the blood of YaShaya; to be made white as snow! Continue to renew, rejuvenate, prepare and revive me in your mighty son's name. Rain down your blessings of wisdom and continue to fill me with Her. Rain down as I know you are about to; Abundance, financially, spiritually, and physically. All good things made to follow. I receive the power you are releasing unto me. Thank you for calling me from where I was. I will wait on you Ahayah, for YaShaya's reign. Keep my thoughts, actions, plans, and goals according to your will only. For no weapon formed against me shall prosper in the name of YaShaya!

Ahayah has instructed me through the reading of Matthew 6:16, to begin a fast.

- Why should I fast?
- How frequent should I?
- May I include my family or is this only for me?
- What aspect of my spiritual self am I benefiting by this fast?

These are actual questions that I wrote down and asked during that time in my quest. There will be more throughout the book. Ahayah answers, you listen and be obedient. Shalawam and head over to the next chapter. It's about to get REAL!

# Chapter 3

## The Things For Which We Pray

Keep Us Ahayah,

From our sinful ways. Humble Us and sustain Us. Silence Us before responding that We may hope to hear from You through your Spirit, the words to be spoken. Keep Us Ahayah, In patience and in peace; In truth and in spirit. Govern Our lives YaShaya and grant Us the words to speak unto all who inquire of us. In the name of YaShaya.

Thank You Father! Thank you for the sweet, juicy grapes in the wilderness. Thank You for every test and for every reminder of humility. Also, thank you for every moment of peace and forgiving our sins. You love Us and you always show it even in discipline. I pray that you continue to provide and protect as well as sustain us in the face of our enemies. Thank you that even when those negative thoughts and lies enter that because of your love and protection, they must eventually flee from us . I pray in the name of YaShaya that every enemy spiritual and physical be silenced and muted, that our ears will be deafened to the conning mischievous lies of Satan. I pray that you begin to mend, heal and restore our hearts and all of our relationships. Deliver us from bondage labeled "the past ", hurt, anger, pain, frustration, sadness, sorrow, self-sabotage by our own ignorance and also from those that we inflict upon others as well. Teach us and show us the way to go, Father. All of these things I pray with thanksgiving as your daughter In YaShaya's mighty and powerful name, Amen!

Have you ever thought about something and had a strong feeling that what you were thinking was right, but wasn't able to prove it? If not, this chapter will definitely shed some light on those types of experiences. For instance, did you know that Abraham Africanus Lincoln was a brown-skinned man? Yes, that means that we had a black president before Obama. I did some digging and found several pictures of him in his childhood, his parents, and his family tree. This was also confirmed later by Elder Rooter's teachings on a live GOCC stream. Why would people work so hard to hide a powerful man's skin color and nationality? Why wouldn't America want this to be known? Perhaps because It would give us hope to know that a president that freed the slaves was a Negro. They went to great lengths to cover this. This is the same as what they are doing right now and have been doing for many years prior. The same thing that the Romans and Greeks did to keep us from knowing the truth about YaShaya. In fact, They just passed a bill that allows Negro and Native American history to be taken out of the school curriculum. Why would they do that? Hmmm...Maybe it has to do with the fact that we are now reading more and want to know our history. Another thing that comes to mind on this subject is the fact that they have manipulated people into believing that King James, Yes; You read that right. King James VI and I were the same person and also a negro. They have even begun to kill off the elders of the Negro community in hopes that they won't be here to give us answers when we begin to ask questions. When I first found out, I wanted to know what Ahayah wanted me to do with this information. Well, Now I know. It is a very interesting position to be in, I must say. Although, It is very rewarding to receive the answers for which I seek; At times, It can be overwhelming. Every man will eventually break. The man who is to be regenerated will be furnished with everything that will serve a means before and during the regeneration. Goods of the affections for the will and also truths from the Word of Ahayah will be given along with confirmations of other sources for excavating understanding. Until, We are furnished with those things; We cannot be regenerated. Those things are food or substance. The interesting thing is that each person will have their own peculiar "food" and it will be provided for them by Ahayah before the regeneration. Shouldn't we rejoice to know that before we take our birthright we will be given the tools needed to rule?

    After waking up at 1:11 am one night, I fell back asleep and began to dream. This was a big deal considering the fact that I have always dreamed meaningful things even since a child. My mom said I was a dreamer and as I got older feared that I may have been detached from reality. There was always something important hidden in my dreams though or so I thought. At this specific time, I hadn't been able to remember a dream in months. Anyhow, I entered into the dream realm and I was in an unfamiliar house inhabited by a European family. Stylez was there with me. The family had a daughter close in age with me and It seemed as if I knew her well or just felt a strange welcoming embrace from her. We sat and talked at an old-fashioned round glass table in her kitchen. Meanwhile, Stylez made himself comfortable in the family's living room; watching television. There was liquor somewhere in the room as well; I'm sure. This dream didn't even appear to be a nightmare until the end. When I went into the girl's parent's bedroom alone once it was time to leave. The parents reminded me of the parents in the Jordan Peele movie called "Get Out." *(It was a movie about an interracial couple visiting the girlfriend's racist parents, who were pretending to be cool and not racist. Although, they were really evil, envious and manipulative. There is so much hidden truth in that movie and It gets really deep but, let's get back to the dream. )* The mother and father both followed behind me shortly after I entered their room. I began to search for something. Although, It was as if I were actually searching for nothing at all. I bent over to look under the lounge sofa in front of their room window and the father made an aggressive sexual pass at me. It was as if my dream self enjoyed this enchantment, but I could feel the real me disapprove and panic. (This was a weird realization in itself. There were two versions of me and both were conscious and aware with two different personalities or perspectives) This of course, represented a battle of good and evil. My dream self seemed to embrace this forbidden sexuality and enticement while the real me was able to take over and pull it back together. This angered my dream self, as if she were actually lusting to participate in this "beltane" ritual . This was sinful and evil. I could feel the battle between the real me and my dream self. Soon, I realized the mother and father were directly behind me , vigorously moving. At this time my dream self was absent; I assume because I gained full control and began to apologize to the parents for being in their room in the first place. When I tried to leave, fear overcame my entire being. I then noticed the prism-shaped crystals hanging from both of their necks. One of the father's crystals was labeled with a yellow stripe around it. I remember thinking, this was placed there purposely. I had once been familiar with those crystals and many more. I knew how to use them and what they stood for. Many of the pagans would use crystals for healing and protective properties; being used in good and bad works but even the good use of something bad is still bad. That was the part that put it all together. These were all the temptations of my past. My sins, iniquities, practices, lustfulness, constant ignorance of danger, glutton, and plenty others. The dream was ended by the real me gaining full control as the daughter walked into the room, almost as if it were timed. That's when it dawned on me. This was all a set up. I had to wake up to save the real me and Stylez who was last seen in the living room. I had hoped he hadn't been subdued by sin and lost the battle. I later went searching for the meaning of the dream and found myself falling into another snare; another form of witchcraft. I started with each item that I could recall seeing in the dream and what they have been said to symbolize. *DISCLAIMER* I do not advise anyone reading to go out and try to interpret dreams. It is dangerous and we must not be ignorant to Satan's devices. According to the heathen crystals are said to represent immunity to criticism or instruction. They can also reflect a naive level of faith in something being perfect. That was almost the perfect description of my relationship with Stylez; but I had to see if we could beat the odds. In other cases, they also represent rebellion or living according to one's own will. Honestly, both seemed completely accurate and could be applied. The appearance of them in a dream suggests clarity or breaking through to higher levels of consciousness. This was definitely happening right before my eyes; Or so I thought. Next, I analyzed each crystal by their color. The European girl was white or caucasian which is used to represent drugs. That would be my pasts' addictions and temptations. The old-fashioned glass round table represented a good time. However sitting at one conveyed a different meaning. Life would be full of pleasant encounters with those who make you feel special. So, this could easily be just a reminder to enjoy the moments you have with your loved ones. Now, this one sounded a little fortune cookie-ish. There also were other meanings behind the table. Honesty, loyalty, and warning that someone close to you deceives you in ways unimaginable. I want you to remember that last meaning for a later part of my journey. The mother and father represent fear of responsibility, unexpressed feelings and also can mean that you are seeking a level of stability in your life. Parents are symbolic of power in a dream. They can also represent an imminent change that is about to happen in your life. This is a sign that we need to prepare and embrace it immediately as it is beneficial. There is one more meaning symbolic for the father. Something about your life that you do not know or haven't accepted yet. There is so much more to a dream than what we often think. Let's go a little deeper. I found that being embraced by the stranger symbolizes being gossiped about. This conveys that we should pay attention to the people we trust and spend our time with and also the idea of not accepting something as the truth while we could. Now, the kitchen is a symbol of change or transformation that is about to occur. The living room symbolizes being comfortable in dangerous or obviously wrong situations. In other cases, this would represent being done with the hard part of a situation.

Now, I thought I at least had an idea of what my dream meant but how was I supposed to know that It was all about to actually happen in only a few days. This dream was a combination of things that were running their course in my life and finally, the order would be restored. From here and out we will just refer to this dream as "The unimaginable." That is exactly what was about to happen. Something so painful and heartbreaking was coming but only to transition me into an even more receptive state of mind. Many people don't understand that even those called dream interpreters in the bible, weren't interpreting the dreams themself. Those interpretations were given unto them by The Father Ahayah. There is even a scripture regarding this in the book of Job, chapter 33 verse 15. So this meant one of two explanations. One, the interpretation was given to me as a warning or two, I had accidentally fallen into another trap of divination. With that being said this wasn't the first time I'd dreamed and it actually came to pass. If you experience anything similar, immediately pray and wait for an answer.

## Chapter 4

## The Unimaginable

    It all happened so fast. One day Stylez and I were doing our usual. He'd just gotten off from work. A moving job that he'd invited a friend to work with him on. I stayed in the car during. The assignment was in downtown Fort Worth. We had 3 cigarettes and all of our money went into gas to get there. I sat in the car doing praise & worship and some bible study for the first 2 hours. I then began to clean out the car to kill time. I still had my praise music turned up and was singing along when a tormented woman with face tattoos, skimpy clothes, and glitching eyes approached the passenger side of my car; specifically asking if I had an extra cigarette to spare. By then we only had two left, one was mine and the other was for when Stylez came back to the car, so I responded "honestly I don't have any extra to spare." I won't lie she seemed possessed but I wasn't completely afraid. I realized that the spirits dwelling within her sought an opportunity to inhabit me or possibly anyone other than her but couldn't if I didn't operate in sin. It dawned on me! It was a trick question. She or it or they clearly needed me to lie at that moment. Nevertheless, she walked away. I would never forget those eyes though. By the time Stylez and his friend got off I'd smoked my whole cigarette and left him half of his own. He was a little upset but he said it was okay because he'd just gotten paid and would be buying us each our own pack. We made it back to the hood and posted up in his usual spot on Gannon. He was drinking and enjoying life in the hood and I was sitting in the car singing every song that came on the radio. Stylez came back way more drunk than usual and He had been drinking moonshine. His usual drink was Christian brothers and Hennessy. I was used to him being drunk in the evening but, this was a different type of drunk. This was a sloppy drunk. I can recall us just sitting in the car while talking after he'd come to the car almost out of it. I asked him something that I can't even remember because it was so insignificant. Possibly it was bigger than I thought; because a huge disagreement broke out from nowhere. We rarely raised our voices at each other. We had experienced small arguments and childish break ups but never had we spoken to one another the way we did that night. He got in my face and dared me to say something else and sadly I told him that I hated him. Before I could blink, his hands were around my neck and he had the most sinister smile on his face. I began to silently pray as I watched his eyes glitch. I started to feel like I was suffocating and all the blood was rushing to my head. I couldn't even cry; I just wanted to breathe again. It was over as quickly as it began. We didn't speak afterwards. We just slept but i couldn't stop playing the fight on repeat in my mind. Stylez didn't even remember what happened the next day, but how could I forget? The next day I went with him to work and it seemed everything was back to normal but oh how sadly mistaken I had been. When it was time for him to get off of work we headed back to the hood and posted up. I was just happy that we'd gotten through that situation. After a few hours, Stylez told me he was going to walk to the gas station to get a beer. He was gone much longer than he should have been so I called him. I got no answer and began to worry. Shortly after I called him, there were gunshots. My mind automatically expected the worst and I began to pray and cry. Several hours had gone by and my phone started to act weird again yet, still no sight of Stylez . It began to softly rain and I had to at least try and call again. So, I faced my fear of rain driving and headed to my dad's. Stylez had disappeared around 5 or 6 p.m. and now It was 1 a.m. I was realizing that he didn't want to be reached. I finally understood that the pain I was feeling at that very moment was unimaginable. I called him from my dad's phone regardless of what had become painfully obvious and still no answer. I drove back to where I was parked before Stylez walked out of my life and sat there, crying. I began to pray and ask for rest. That's when suddenly there was thunder and then the rain started falling harder and almost instantly I was asleep. My prayers had been answered. This was the most peaceful sleep I could recall. In the midst of so much pain and confusion; I was being comforted. I woke up the next morning with a horrible cough, puffy eyes and barely a voice. The key words being "I woke up." My phone was still out of commission until it wasn't. It would come back to life long enough to be useful and then out again. I had a show every Friday and Sunday so I had to get it together by the end of the week. It eventually dawned on me. Could "the unimaginable" have been a forewarning of this very thing? If so, then I had to realize that there was more to come. I felt all alone and didn't know what to do. This man had taught me so much even about myself, and we'd shared even our deepest thoughts and ideas. I began to cry again. I had to get better, I had to be healed from this large hole left in my chest where my heart was supposed to be. Only YaShaya himself could fix what was broken. I was the broken thing that needed to be fixed. Everything I had tried to heal myself of was all still lingering, I couldn't do it. My phone had gotten to a point where it had its own schedule and there was nothing that I could do about it. If you can't beat them, join them, right? So I would do my abides, research biblical meanings for words using Strong's concordance and seek wisdom in the bible as much as I could during the function time. The rest of the time I was listening to 101.7 fm and praying. Yet, still I hadn't heard from Stylez. He was M.I.A. and I couldn't afford to be consumed with thoughts of his whereabouts and who with. All I knew was that he wasn't with me and didn't want to be found. The first 2 days I experienced extreme sorrow but, by the third day I was hearing clearly from YaShaya and seeing beauty and signs in his wonders. I was instructed through prayer one morning to begin a fast. I would only consume water and herbs for 7 days. So I did just that. I felt myself merging with the spiritual realm deeply. I began to hear and receive directions and instructions entering into my mind but also creating a vibrational shift in my heart. I was led to places to see and witness things that no one would ever believe and which many wouldn't understand. I was led to realize that Ahayah had me right where he wanted me. I could only depend on him and that was the most crucial point. I was called to return to work at the health food store in Richardson on the second or third day of my fast. I would find myself having physical conversations with YaShaya via his Holy Spirit all throughout the workday. I was healing physically and mentally. YaShaya was purging me through the fast and also setting the stage for a grand entrance.

Fortunately, I made a friend named Bee whom I would sometimes take back and forth to work. She always offered me a spot on her couch and at first I would decline because Stylez wasn't there to protect me. Eventually, I accepted her offer. She would always offer me things like food and extra gas money. Bee was what I believed a true friend should be even through our few disagreements. Bottomline Bee was there for me in dark times. Some might even call her an angel in disguise even if she said the same of me. I knew I was nowhere near. She was just sent at a specific time in my life and in exchange for her friendship, Ahayah blessed her through me as well. We grew close in only a matter of weeks through prayer and spiritual conversation. She even asked me to help her get closer to YaShaya. Who am I for anyone to request such things? Why did people feel inspired by my rededication and transformation? Ahayah had it all mapped out and was undoubtedly about to unveil the masterpieces which he was sculpting, polishing and painting. Bee had a horrible situation going on during this time. She had been tricked into a relationship with a deceitful thief. It wasn't all bad. Eventually, he wound up seeking answers of the true god of Israel. Ahayah used our friendship to deliver Bee from his grasp and to spark interest to bring back one of his sons.

The days were passing by and YaShaya was strengthening me in each of them. I continued to pray and seek the truth, waking up each morning to rise before the sun and give praise before the birds. I accompanied a few friends at an event one night after work. These friends were fellow artists and local promoters. I had such a wonderful time that I'd forgotten the pain and worry of my circumstances until the fun was over. When it was all over and everyone departed I was reminded that I had nowhere to go and I felt it was too late to call Bee. I ended up once again sitting in my car. While parked behind a gas station, I began to pray and then I was led to call one of my promoter friends Hood. I'd known him for years but never exceeded the level of professional associates. He was surprisingly very understanding and welcoming; I was invited to come over and rest until I could reach my dad. He offered me a place to come whenever I was in need and he lived right across the way from Uncle Dee Dee. So as you can see, doors were being opened literally. The Most High was constructing a temporary support system around me and I didn't even realize it. I remember praying to be forgiven for making Stylez an idol and for YaShaya to keep me from doing it again with anyone else. I also remember professing that I only want to trust him and Ahayah for everything I need in life. I thanked YaShaya for everything and then asked for the strength to heal and never sin against He nor The Most High again. That's when it happened. After praise and worship I was greeted by a bird. I decided to test my faith by asking Ahayah if I could have it. Just as I asked, I was greeted by two more and then soon; 40. This certainly brought a deeper understanding to the message portrayed in "Cinderella". I began to praise in song once more only to be joined in worship by every one of the 40 birds. This was so magical. They flew around me in patterns as if they were being orchestrated. I had asked for one and received many. Did you know that birds were also created to glorify Ahayah? They do their job so well. Perhaps, that was another way of being comforted by Ahayah's spirit.

# Chapter 5

# Ashah Chayal

    What a blessing it was to start the day off this way and to know that this was still only the beginning. There were many special things included in this day. It was also my mom's birthday. Of course at the time I hadn't yet known that we shouldn't celebrate birthdays. I hadn't yet known that this was a day of vanity and that the only one worthy of a day of praise is our heavenly Father Ahayah through His son our savior YaShaya. Afterward, I proceeded to prepare for this amazing day. I called my mom and gave her special birthday wishes and then picked out my clothes for the day. Another amazing thing occurred while I was getting dressed. I began to receive instruction on how to dress for this day. It was magical. I was once again being led by the spirit. Everything from the colors down to how my hair should be was given to me. A crown was placed on my head as if I were from a long line of royalty. Before heading to my mom's house I decided to go shopping for a gift. First, I stopped by Bee's house and there I ran into a man inhabited by many demons in disguise. Although, at the time I didn't know it yet. Later, he did reveal himself. He was a friend or one might even say an associate of Bee's boyfriend D.

    While speaking to Bee regarding my mom's birthday the associate whose name will not be spoken, interrupted and told me to wish my mom a happy birthday for him. This was strange but not a bother. He hadn't crossed the line yet. There was something evil about him that I could feel but not pinpoint. He even offered a contribution towards my mom's gift. Although, this gesture seemed kind and generous; I still had to remind him that I wasn't single, just going through something at the moment and not to get the wrong idea. He pretended to understand and agreed. Later, It would be revealed that all money isn't good money. Anyhow, I accepted the money and headed off to do some shopping. I had invited Bee to accompany me but she'd declined since she'd not long gotten off from work. It was so peaceful to know that no matter what I was dealing with YaShaya would cradle me.

After shopping for my mom and grabbing something for myself as well I received a text from Stylez. I still had his clothes in my car and since I was in the process of healing, I offered to bring them to him. I knew that I still loved him and I'd hoped He still loved me, but I figured it would be easier if he had them so I wouldn't be played with or drawn back in to be hurt again. This week felt like a year. So many things had transpired. YaShaya had begun to sort through my broken pieces and put certain ones together to make me new. This will be explained in detail later. Stylez ended up calling after a few texts back and forth.

So, I pulled up thinking that I had the strength to face the man that had seemed to abandon me. I gave him his clothes and I began to cry. I almost thought I was beginning to hate him. Hate is such a strong word but it felt close.

I couldn't understand why this was happening to me. How could the man that made me so happy and played a role in leading me away from a horrible addiction be the same man that broke me down this way? How could he just stand there as if he didn't care? That's when his voice disrupted my spiraling train of thoughts and he asked for a hug. I remember hugging him as tight as I could and not wanting to let go while tears streamed from under my new sunglasses. We hugged for several moments which seemed way longer to me than it actually was. I can remember my body trembling as if something spiritual was occurring and it was, little did I know. I got back in the car and lingered before driving off. Maybe He was right. In one of our texts, He'd told me that this wasn't our season and surely It wasn't.

Not all hope was lost. Soon He'd return but possibly in a different state of mind. First, I had to accept that at this moment I could only control what I had power over and sadly, that wasn't this situation. I went along and headed to my mom's and finally told her what the current state of my relationship with Stylez was. I couldn't stay long but we had a beautiful conversation about Ahayah and YaShaya whose names I hadn't yet known. I had a show later that evening in Plano and then work, the next morning so I left and prepared for bed. YaShaya had spoken to me while at work the next day and told me that I would hear from Stylez again. He didn't say how soon but He did say that it would be soon.

On my lunch break, I left work to obtain a new phone. I had enough of these phone issues! So I went to Boost Mobile and while seeking an android I came across a marked-down iPhone 8. This was an upgrade from the one I had. Even with it being marked down I ended up not having enough to pay the cost of taxes and an extra month's bill. I was just about to give up and take the android when I was led to call my mom and my little sister Lexi. "Abundance" I heard. They both sent money towards my new phone and I still didn't have enough. The reason was that the store clerk had quoted me the wrong discounted price but Ahayah stepped in and urged her in a miraculous way. She took off $100 of the cost and added it to a deduction from her next paycheck. Things like this don't happen every day.

I was beginning to understand that The Most High Ahayah favored me and I would never know why. I returned to work almost an hour late but wasn't reprimanded nor lectured. This definitely was His favor. I initially thought to tell an exaggerated lie about traffic and a long line at the store but was urged by the spirit that in telling the truth I would be protected. It worked! I was simply instructed and briefed for the next project and began with no issues. While working I had several more conversations with the spirit of YaShaya. These talks made the day go by so much faster. I was overcome with joy and being taught to solely depend on Christ. When I got off while walking with a coworker to my car I got a text from Stylez. It read "Hey queen how are you doing?" I remember feeling at least 3 different emotions at once. I finally responded after calming down.

    We texted for a while along the drive home and we made a date to meet. Although, he didn't show up nor call; It was okay. I was disappointed but not heartbroken this time. That night I had agreed to take Bee to work and sleep at her house until it was time to pick her up for work. Things would hardly go as planned. I awoke and prepared to go pick up Bee that morning but she had called to tell me she was going to take an Uber. So, I went out on the patio. I figured that I might as well do my morning bible study and worship. While on the balcony praying, I was once again interrupted by a familiar voice. It was Stylez looking up at me with that charming smile. How could I stay mad? He told me he was going to the store and that he would be coming upstairs afterward. He never returned though. I think I had begun to expect disappointment from him. I had gotten dressed and was getting ready to leave when We ran into each other directly under the tree where we first fell in love. How strange, right? I know, but not as strange as this next part. I recall Bee telling me that Stylez and I would have the greatest love story of All time. I am not sure about the "of all time" part, but Ahayah did so much through our story in such a short time.

## Chapter 6

## Under The Tree

There was still work being done on us both but this was the beginning of something. We spent the day together and then I dropped him off. I was so happy to be back together. This was a spiritual battle that was won and there would be many more. I slept well that night and the next day I went to the park. I was following a trail of numbers and their Hebrew meanings according to the Strong's concordance. I ended up on the phone with my mom while there. She was starting to see what was happening to me. That was a relief because now I knew I wasn't going crazy and that it all made sense to someone else. I showed her everything that I'd been seeing and told her most of what I'd heard. She too found it amazing and a blessing of favor from the Most High. While we were on the phone I journeyed into the woods near the park and showed her that this is where I felt I was being led. I put her on FaceTime so that she could see for herself. This was one of the most amazing experiences yet! I laid my bible and purple book down on the ground in front of a beautiful purple bush. Just as I kneeled to the ground with my arms up, I felt a hand grab my arm as if to hold my hand up. I remember telling my mom that I could feel someone holding my hand when my shadow caught my attention. It was no longer my shadow! It had transformed into A short woman wearing a crown and that's when It happened. I was still on FaceTime so my mom witnessed the transformation of my shadow also. Then, at the exact same time we both realized and knew who it was. My mom shouted " Brandi, It looks like Granny!" That is literally when the phone disconnected and died. I knew what I'd seen, but how? How could my mom and I have both seen my grandmother Gloria Jean Van after being passed over for more than 12 years. There was no scientific explanation. Only Ahayah could perform such a miracle and only YaShaya could reveal the plans before it even happened. He even warned me that I'd lose my keys trying to get to the car so quickly and that too came to pass. I kept thinking back to the moment where peace suddenly transformed into fear. Ahayah did not give us the spirit of fear so I knew this feeling was cast by Lucifer in an attempt to throw me out of focus. I had become so focused on The Most High and wanting to find the truth in all that he has for me. This angered the enemy. I was slowly putting down all childish things, well almost all of them. One childish characteristic would play an important role in this discovery filled journey and that was me discovering and gaining the ability to exhibit childlike faith. I had to be willing to learn and follow my father no matter where he took me. Little did I know just how far He was about to take me . When I left I sat in the car for hours. I had no one to run to and I couldn't shake that spirit of fear until the next sunrise. I remember sitting in the car praying for YaShaya to remove the spirit of fear from me and to forgive me for running. I pleaded that my running didn't make me like Jonah in the bible. The Most High gave me peace again but the enemy kept coming against me to convict and burden my heart. I was led to analyze the cause of my fear and suddenly it began to make sense. I was at first unsure if I had done something sinful or evil which led to seeing my grandmother. That's when Ahayah taught me that when people so called "die" they are not dead at all.  Yes, they lose their physical bodies but their spirit never dies. Later, I was also shown where we pass on to and the construction of the resting place for those who lived a truly good life and those who chose sin. This is also taught in scripture during the times of Christ walking the earth and Lazarus' encounter with death. In conclusion, nothing is impossible on earth because nothing is impossible for Ahayah nor YaShaya. People would think that me not eating during the days of the fast could have driven me to insanity but, no. Not eating allowed my body to be purged and purified. This possibly opened a spiritual portal to aid in my receiving of heavenly information. I hadn't become invincible but with all of this information and these new methods of thinking, I became prepared for whatever would come next.

## Chapter 7

## Wisdom the Beloved

I could have gone back to Bee's or even to my uncle's house to take a nap. However, I wound up at the park being rudely awakened from my amazingly peaceful rest by the ring of my phone. On the other end was Stylez. He was yelling and talking angrily at me about lies that he was told by those same deceitful demons inhabiting the man who'd offered me money towards my mom's birthday gift. I strongly felt the anger transferring into me from him. Needless to say that feeling of rest was no longer with me. I was reminded of a scripture I'd been led to read and take notes on a couple of weeks back. "Matthew 18:15-17" As I was led back to it again, I began to realize exactly why I had it referenced in the first place. I had already been given the method of calmly settling this issue. When we have a conflict with our brother or sister first, tell them one on one how their actions against you hurt. If they do not listen, take one or two witnesses along with you so that each charge may be established by their evidence as well. After that, If they refuse to listen go and tell it to the church. Lastly, If they still refuse then they shall be as a gentile unto you. Remembering the steps, I immediately drove over to Bee's house to get to the bottom of it and to my surprise she played a role in these false accusations. I was hurt by my friend and she knew the truth so after speaking with her in a one on one confrontation she came to apologizing and repented of her betrayal. Next, I went to confront Nameless. We will call him that because he shall remain nameless. We confronted him together on his front porch. Not disrespectfully but firm and supported by facts. I remember while speaking to him the look of guilt on his face. Yet, He continued to lie so I began to state the facts of the situation which he'd twisted and distorted. Finally, He'd admitted the truth and agreed to tell Stylez the truth but at this point I wouldn't dare allow him to speak on my behalf. I remembered as I walked away, that weeks before when Stylez was gone I'd written about a demon with no name. How he'd have a smile full of deceit and in his eyes were truths that would be twisted and bent to cause conforming and condemnation. Ahayah had shown me a few things about demons and how they would want to conquer our minds and use the people around us to do it. It felt good to stand firm, hold my ground, and trust YaShaya to do the rest. Even after all of the chaos I would forgive because I refused to let any anger or hurt drag me into darkness and away from all that Ahayah was building in me. I forgave Bee, said goodbye and headed down Highway 67 towards my uncle Dee's house. When I pulled up my cousin was outside walking her dog CoCo. Everyone loves CoCo. She is a caramel mocha bully with a wet nose and a kind spirit; unless she sensed danger . Then, you might want to dip as fast as possible; if you are the danger.I began to tell her what had just happened and how crazy it was but also the way that Ahayah had given me the plan to solve the situation. As we were talking, Hood pulled up and invited me to a photo shoot downtown. This studio was amazing. I began to do a photo opt of my own while there. It was such a good experience that I wasn't even bothered by the events that took place earlier. Stylez called eventually and I filled him in on what all went down. I was glad to hear from him and noticed a change in his demeanor. I told him I love him and that I was leaving a pop up photoshoot downtown. I thought that was the end of the amazing day until Hood told me that we were heading to a place called "Turkey Dam". This place was unlike any restaurant/club I'd ever seen. We weren't there for the food though. Turkey Dam featured a locally famous Dj from 67.5 the jam and we were there to hire her for the upcoming fashion show that I'd been invited to perform in. Initially, I thought that Hood would be doing the talking and negotiating. Soon I realized that was never the plan. Once we spotted Dj Daisia T, Hood insisted that I speak to her and so I did. She had a crowd of people around her so I had to be bold. I signaled for one of the waitresses who'd messed up my order earlier and asked her if she'd do me the favor of asking the Dj to come speak with me. I couldn't believe how simple it was and she came right away. I told her about the fashion show and that I'd be performing there as well. She put her number in my phone because the music was loud and we could barely hear each other. I felt so accomplished in having completed my task. About a week later, Ahayah showed me that a joining or espousing was soon to be in order. This was confirmed several times during my writings, reading and research. Of course, I initially assumed that joining was Stylez and I; But it was not. I will say this and that is Only Ahayah could arrange the order of events that were about to happen next.

    Transformation is the topic. What is it really? When people go into a bathroom looking decent and come out looking amazing? Is it turning a bowl of peeled apples into a scrumptious apple pie? We assume that transformation is something we can do on our own. However, It truly takes a miracle from Ahayah to transform. He is the only one who can truly take a person of doubts, fears and pain to transform them into a person of truth, freedom and peace. How do I know? That person was once me, remember? Although the transformation is still in progress I can honestly say that I was chosen by The Most High to be used for edification of His people. As a child, I'd always felt different like I didn't belong because I didn't. I know that now but, I was once weak and trying to fit in. Now looking back I can understand why. I have always been known for the musical talents Ahayah gave me even back then. When is it okay to look back? Think about that before we go into this eighth chapter...

## Chapter 8

## Walk By Faith

One night while staying over to Bee's with Stylez. I arose and went outside to the balcony as usual. The sun had begun to come up. I grabbed my purse which contained my blessed oil, bible, purple book of quests and some gathered herbs. I went out and began my morning prayer and preparation. I thought about how on the night before Bee and I held our own personal bible study. We tapped into "The Book of Nehemiah" chapter 7. It was amazing! We began after Bee cooked dinner. Although, not before a small altercation broke out between Bee and her boyfriend D. It soon turned into an even bigger altercation between D and I. No worries though, YaShaya swooped in and battled on my behalf. So in the beginning, I walked into the apartment to find Bee and D yelling at each other. YaShaya had shown me this would occur while I was on my way up the stairs. So obviously there was no surprise when it came true. Unsure of what to do, I paused and thought to myself "think fast!" Honestly, I didn't have to because the Spirit intervened. I was given the words to softly de-escalate and help usher in self-conviction. The Spirit did the rest. The words I was given were used to remind Bee that she wasn't alone and that I'd experienced her current emotions many times in my life. I now understood that I had to in order to get to this point. She eventually became calm and that is when I lured her out to the patio away from the source of her anger. The balcony was peaceful even in the midst of chaos. The enemy had to flee for being subdued by YaShaya's peace. Immediately after Bee and I had exited to the balcony, D had gone to lay down and swiftly fallen asleep.

Bee and I had a beautiful worship which of course led to prayer and so much revelation.

Also, Stylez had truly returned. This time something so beautiful and profound was occurring. I thought that the enemy had began to lose all power which once allowed him to influence our relationship; later I would find that not to be true though. Stylez and I were led to our usual water place. This was the second time. It wouldn't be until next year that the secrets of the water places would be revealed to me. I brought along with me my blanket, bible and oil. Stylez was led to fish out something that appeared to be a book in the distant waters. Stylez then broke off a twig from the tall Egyptian looking grass nearby. He used it to navigate the mysterious book towards the edge of the water where we stood. Eventually, Stylez came to possess it but, It wasn't a book. Once it was fished out we could see that it was only a leaf. How could a leaf look like a thick book? How could we have both seen the same illusion? We ended up wrapping the leaf around a "Y" shaped stick and placing it on the ground near a tree which cast shade upon us. Just then, I was led away from our picnic area towards another but bigger "Y" shaped stick which was planted deeply in the ground. We knew somehow these were signs, but from who or what? We were having a hard time discerning the works of Ahayah and the snares of Lucifer. We were then led to take a stick which lay near the water on the shore. It was as if it had been washed upon the shore. Laying eyes upon it we were both given an instinct. "Place it into the water." So We did. Suddenly, the water began to flow up to the top of the stick instead of downwards. I remember thinking "Slowly He has begun transforming the man that I love into A humble man by His grace."

A great Hebrew woman once said "A woman's heart must be so lost in Ahayah that any man who seeks it must seek Ahayah first to find it." This was so true and profound. Our love would never be perfect ,but maybe this was a sign that there was hope for our future together. Later that night, We had a performance. Stylez and I had been drinking. I hadn't drank in quite a while but I was tempted and took two shots. We immediately found ourselves under the spirits of anger and confusion. We were at a club in Addison, TX called "The Volume Lounge." While there I felt something different than my usual turn up. I received an epiphany which allowed me to get a more clear understanding of the history of nightclubs and parties. These were originally places for ritualistic, unholy practices. I was awakening to every truth and given answers to any question I had asked. Knowing the truth about things definitely changes your perception of them. That is the gift of wisdom, I believe. I was ready to go but the show must go on. I was using the gifts that The Most High had given me the wrong way. All I wanted to do from then on was to spread his word and love throughout the world. Soon it was time for me to go on. I rocked it and even had the audience singing along with me. This feeling was all I'd longed for for years and now It seemed vain. I once loved the spotlight but this felt wrong. I could hear the cheers and clapping but I was now able to see I had become a pawn of the enemy in creating stumbling blocks with my lyrics. The song I performed was called "They ain't ready". It glorified profane language, the use of crystals, and other sinful practices. Clearly, when I wrote it ; I wasn't ready. After I performed we greeted several fans and then left. Still drunk, the arguing started again and we continued to argue and fight on the way back to Bee's house. During an intermission of this emotional battle, I was led to realize there was a spirit symbolized by a frog(another unclean creature) attacking us both. I began to pray and renounce it's power. Surely, YaShaya heard me because soon we were granted peace. Although several stones were cast, compassion and wisdom sailed on in . By the time we'd arrived at Bee's house it was all over and we'd both grown tired and sleepy.

After falling asleep a vision was given to me . A vision of fire or a coal like substance raining from the Heavens. The whole world in the dream was dark. There was no sun and people of all kinds were just running around screaming. I wasn't exactly sure what to take from this but, I also wasn't afraid. The next morning I arose early, mistaking that Bee would need me to pick her up from work. I could definitely use the extra rest and I honestly felt that was exactly what The Most High was urging me to do. So, I lay back down and once again found myself wrapped tightly in Stylez' loving, protective arms. At this time I was still lukewarm and oblivious to the sin being committed on a daily basis. Hours later we were both awake and no longer alone. Bee's boyfriend was home and already starting his usual instigative practices. He'd turned on the television and placed it on a viral youtube channel where the content was Egyptian, anti-Christ doctrine. After a small disagreement, I received instructions to de-escalate the issue accordingly. It was made clear to me that this man had been confused by false teachings and condemnation over time. This was the source of his lack of faith. I had a feeling this would soon change but I'm no fortune teller. That would all depend on Ahayah's plan and timing. Anyhow, we ended it with love and compassion. Next, Stylez and I were dressed and parted from D. Once we were in the car Stylez looked at me and asked "Where do you want to go bae?" Immediately, I knew where I wanted to go. I remembered where it was already written. I answered and said "When you get to the light on Camp Wisdom and Cockrel Hill go right." I followed with a statement "Don't be afraid or freaked out by anything we might be about to encounter." He looked at me and agreed. We were led to a place in the wilderness. This was the same place where I'd seen my grandmother. Being led was becoming the usual for us both now. Once, behind the park we entered into the wilderness. The pages of my purple notebook began turning by the force of the wind. They were being turned to specific sections of my book. As if those specific sections were written to be read aloud. The pages were prayers that I'd written weeks before. Soon it was made known that we were not alone. Afterwards, we headed back to the water place.

On this trip to the water we again experienced something miraculous. The most High had provided us with a few uniquely significant coins. This reminds me of the coins or in Greek "drachma" appearing in the fishes' mouth when the man was in need of money to pay taxes. YaShaya told him to pay his also. Each of our coins had a specific picture on the back. Each coin was different and held a message or a clue of the quest we hadn't known we'd be soon embarking on. One of them depicted a great white swan on a "Y" shaped branch. We had no clue how many amazing things we were about to witness. This picture would soon be a physical manifestation before our eyes. When We arrived there were two ducks in the pond and then we were made aware of a rare beautiful bird at a distance in the tall Egyptian-like grass. Unknowingly, Stylez made a powerful statement that would soon resonate. This statement was about to come to pass. The rare white beautiful bird was just minding her business, unbothered. That's when Stylez and I were scoped out by two snakes in the water. They swam so fast and seemingly they were trying to get to us. I'd never seen anything like it. These snakes were literally trying to get to us. I believe the great white bird was a manifestation of The Most High's spirit. Suddenly the beautiful bird took flight. She flew close to us and spread her large heavenly wings. She wanted us to see her and pay attention to what she would do next. She turned around and swooped both snakes out of the water. Then, she proceeded to land on the other end of the water, right on a "Y" shaped branch. I grabbed the coin and reminded Stylez of the image printed on it. We had literally just witnessed a miracle. I realized that Stylez' statement from before "She was waiting and protecting her children." The children were us! How amazing this was and it wasn't even over. We took this as a sign that it was time to leave though. So we headed towards the ramp to the car. While walking towards the ramp, we encountered a big bright red cardinal. How wonderful and profound? We had witnessed 2 rare beautiful birds one after the other. It's song was so beautiful and hard to ignore. We finally made it to the car and just as it was in sight, a lovely blue mocking bird swooped in front of us and landed on the branch diagonal to where our car was parked. Wow! All we could do was give praise to The Most High for the beauty of his creations and his never ending protection upon us. We had just witnessed 3 amazing creations of The Creator. This was deeper than just seeing birds though. We felt as if we'd just been visited by the presence of The Heavenly Father Ahayah, His wife The Holy Spirit and The son Yashaya by the manifestation of birds. This was a form of theophany, protection, confirmation and increase of faith.

Following all of the excitement, Stylez desired to go and shoot some hoops. He wanted to show me the place he would once go to clear his mind and relieve his stress. So off to Duncanville we went. This was a place I had never been but had seen in passing by. There were young teenage boys playing basketball on one side and an empty court on the other. One section of the land was occupied by easter egg hunt participants. Easter's hidden truths had been revealed to me as well. A time of rituals and sacrifices unto the Babylonian goddess Ishtar or Ashtaroth. She was also known as Isis and the spirit of Nimrod's mother; The Evil Semiramis. She was also known as the "queen mother of heaven" and the goddess of fertility &love. We blocked out the pagan ritual in process and proceeded towards the empty court. Stylez began to shoot the basketball, making every shot. I was intrigued and I began to video and take pictures. He was pretty good and that wasn't a shock to me. We were soon accompanied by a seemingly bored young man in search of fellowship. I was sure he'd just found it. I immediately knew this was an assignment and Stylez agreed. I soon understood it was an assignment for Stylez and not I. I watched them shoot for a few and then I headed to the car. While in the car, I continued to watch. The young boy started out with a lack of confidence. I watched and admired Stylez' coaching of the young man. He soon began to make his shots effortlessly. Stylez had completed his task in excellence. When He'd returned to the car, We headed to my mother's house in Midlothian.

## Chapter 9

## Blessings in Things Unseen

It had been quite a while since we'd visited my mom together. We used to go once a week and Stylez would grill. This visit was the most pleasant visit. We stayed about two hours although I may be mixing up my days on this part. The Almighty's presence truly was near and we were provided with several signs and wonders. I had gotten into the habit of sharing this new found wisdom and faith with my mother. Heaven was the destination and earth was the departure. There were moments where I felt she needed more convincing or proof and that was fine. I completely understand that we were to test and prove all things. Though, even the smallest doubts and questions would soon be addressed. The Most High was unveiling both of our eyes slowly. While at my moms I received all of the mail she'd put up for me. There were three letters and one of them was about to answer a big prayer for us and bless two of my children. It would even address the concerns of their father. The treasure was divided into three parts and distributed amongst us, my daughter Noni and my son Kai'Lel. I promised to consult YaShaya on where and how our portion would be spent. I was confident that it would be multiplied in His Holy name. I was in awe of all the things my father was doing and Him keeping us in His will. The Almighty then led us to a hotel in Lancaster.

This was a new place which he laid us away. We were hidden in plain sight and the peace of Christ befell us. It was just a blessing to not sleep in the car nor on someone's couch, even if only one night. The next day, we would link up with my dear old friend Cory also known as Global Don and Don Tex. He and Stylez locked in quickly, having met for the first time. We ended up pulling out our bibles and having a passionate bible study session after leaving the studio. We even stayed until I grew tired and sleepy but the mission was complete and the music we created was beautiful. Stylez fed me fish for dinner and we ended up staying the night in Plano at a different hotel. There in the room we encountered a few demonically influenced disputes. The spirit of love and peace prevailed in those trials as well. I will continue to stress the importance of keeping faith, being obedient and thinking strategically in war. We must be mindful of the tools used by the enemy as well as those provided by our Heavenly Father Ahayah.

These particular trials were a lesson from which we gained much wisdom and knowledge. We had been at the Magnuson when we entered into a long night of restlessness and arguing. There was no apparent reason for the arguing, we just suddenly grew frustrated with one another. This was clearly demonic. We eventually were able to overcome the anger and mend what was being harmed in our relationship. Upon falling asleep, I entered into the dream realm where I encountered a mute demon that frightened me all throughout my childhood. He was always on a mission to kill but something amazing occurred this time. He was weak and powerless this time around but that didn't stop him from trying. The dream made sense suddenly. The enemy is powerless over us but he chases and attacks in the ways he can hoping that we will show fear to empower him. The epiphany was that now he'd lost the power of frightening us with the chase. The next morning We received a call from our brother S.O.G which woke us. He was eager and excited, inviting us to his home in Georgia. We accepted feeling this would be the leap of faith that would change our lives.

We were scheduled to leave the upcoming Sunday and his fiancé had just left a few days before. I believed that if it was true love that she would soon return just as Stylez had. Anyways, the time to go forth had arrived and that meant that we would go up and out of our "Land of Bondage." I believed that Texas could no longer hold us in captivity now that YaShaya had arranged our freedom and ascension.

The day of departure had arrived. I went unto YaShaya to pray to Ahayah and was led by the Holy Spirit into study. This was a powerful rising and the worship and praise that followed lasted for hours. After getting dressed and packed, My mother called and was on her way to see us off. She stopped and got me a mango smoothie, which was my favorite flavor and also it coordinated with the fast of only fruits and vegetables i was partaking in. We followed her to the gas station and filled up our tank for the quest ahead. We said our "see ya laters" then we were off to spread the word in obedience; I thought. We saw several confirmations from Ahayah while traveling for fifteen exciting hours. We noticed everything from numbers, city signs, birds, exit numbers, buildings, obtaining more coins, shadows of beautiful images and the soft whispers of the Holy spirit as well. We smiled at one another and agreed that this was a beautiful new beginning.

## Chapter 10

## Still Standing

I received a phone call from my mom's number but it definitely wasn't my mom. The person on the other end of the phone was Miss Princess, a friend of my mom's. She wanted to tell me about a powerful mission she'd been invited to be a part of and that she wanted to include me. This resonated with a vision I was given back in 2019. That was the year I was run over by a car and left for dead on Highway I-35 & Parkerville in Desoto on July 4th. Miraculously by the grace of Ahayah I survived. Broken clavicle bone, two fractured ribs and a broken pelvic bone. The enemy once again failed at claiming my life. He never wanted nor expected me to make it this far. This far meaning, far enough to discover the truth about Christ and my own identity. It was becoming clear that YaShaya had important plans for me. All of those injuries and I was able to walk in two or three days. What a blessing! I knew that my father loved me without a doubt.

We'd been in Georgia about a week before we made a visit to Atlanta. A friend of S.O.G's named Eric had a birthday. We rolled out to celebrate with him. We left later than planned and there was a small disagreement on who's car to take. I thought we should all just ride in Stylez and I's car but as we all know a hard head makes a soft "You know what." S.O.G had become like our brother, when in truth; the enemy wanted to use him to break me. Soon that all would be revealed. I tried to overlook his reactions towards my intimacy with YaShaya but eventually it was hard not to notice. The spirits that inhabited him became angry with me and my constant praise and worship. I reminded myself that everything has its purpose. Our two hour drive quickly became a five to six hour drive when S.O.G's car caught a flat right outside of Albany. Stylez immediately got out to help while I began calling tire shops in the area. Stylez put on the spare and I located a near tire shop.

    All of this had occurred and I wondered if S.O.G had realized that this was no coincidence. We ended up pulling up at Walmart and getting a tire. The whole time we were waiting I was in praise and worship mode. We finally made it to Atlanta and arrived at the studio. Once we got into the parking lot we were greeted by Vyzion. He was one of S.O.G's nephews and also the engineer we'd be working with. He was very talented and had a deep passion for what he was doing but, He was slightly arrogant. Honestly, at times so was I. With me, S.O.G. Vyzion, and Stylez in the lab there was bound to be friction. Too many brilliant minds and creative flows at once! Needless to say , the session was a success; despite a few small back to back disagreements in the subject of religion and truth. Vyzion wasn't mean. He was just overly confident and blunt in an almost annoying way. However, it all ended peacefully. The Most High eventually intervened and revealed to me what the enemy was actually trying to keep from occurring. There was something about Vyzion and I had hoped that we would work again in the future. It was funny because he said the things that someone would think but not be brave enough to say. I thought it was hilarious how he annihilated the topic of the song. I was actually featured on S.O.G's daughters' song. My entire verse was a clever twist to the song's original concept but when i finished recording Vyzion goes " Y'all really made a song about Xannies in the middle of an opioid epidemic"? Why hadn't we thought about that though. Anyways, Over the next few days nothing really significant occurred. It's important to remember that even as a family we are all still human. People have gotten away from discussing things. There will always be times when we have to agree to disagree or need space. Overall, we must be merciful towards one another and continue to respond in love. I knew from experience , that was easier said than done.

    The following Friday we got up and dressed to go to the store. When we returned S.O.G had locked the door and was pulling out of the driveway when we were pulling in. We even blew the horn and called his phone but he didn't answer. Here we were 15 hours away from everyone we knew locked out and being ignored by the only person we trusted in the state of Georgia. At first there was anger boiling inside of us both but, soon it transformed into determination and drive. We headed to the DFCS office immediately. I filled out an application for food stamps, TANF and medicaid. We needed to establish some stability and that meant we needed to utilize the offered resources. The spirit led and I was confident that The Most High had already begun his work in our favor. Next we drove around the corner to the Albany Georgia Dept of Housing. When I got out I couldn't find the door but I was focused and determined to accomplish these things in one day. With the grace and mercy of Ahayah how could I fail. Once I arrived at the housing authority window, I met a woman named Mylesha.  She had given me a sticky note with the phone number of Ms. Tevelyn written on it and she had also instructed me to call her after 2pm. Before I left I began to feel an urge from the Holy Spirit. So I obeyed and asked her if I may pray with her. Mylesha consented. I hadn't known what she was going through but Ahayah knew. She was grateful for the prayer and I was happy to serve my father's command. When I called Ms. Tevelyn didn't answer but I did leave her a message. Eventually, I called again and got her on the phone that time. She conducted my initial and second screening by phone. She went from being cold and strict to suddenly someone I could tell The Most High had placed in my corner. That day I learned to call things under the subjection of YaShaya and into alignment of Ahayah's will. That is exactly what I began to do. I knew that we were just on the brink of receiving many blessings.

The next morning after a peaceful rest, I was visited by another blue bird. It was the start of a day full of fun and excitement. Until evening fell and offenses were made then reconciled. Also, a prayer was offered up and once again peace was restored. That night, Stylez stayed up while I slept and I arose around 6:27 am. He'd literally just fallen asleep. I got out of bed and prepared for my usual morning praise and worship. Heading out the door I leaned over and gently kissed Stylez on the lips. I was reminded that all things work together for the good of those who love Ahayah. I still hadn't yet grasped the fact that we were steadily operating in sin. Soon, I would though.

## Chapter 11

## Grapes in the Wilderness

    Over the next few days the enemy became relentless in his attacks. There were multiple fights between S.O.G and I separate from the ones with Stylez and I. I was constantly and consistent in prayer and faith but that doesn't mean we won't go through things. It means we have to stay grounded and trust in YaShaya. Soon, It was time for me to leave this temporary place and It grieved me to once again not be able to share a bed with Stylez; but this too would only be temporary. I was still in Georgia just a few minutes away. Zakar "The unimaginable",I was forewarned and prepared yet still that didn't keep me from crying. I'd learned that I was gossiped about by people that I loved and thought loved me. This was another slandering attack and as long as Christ remained as my focus I would not be defeated.

    After 10 hours of prayer and tears Ahayah miraculously provided a roof over my head and a safe place to rest. I'd met a man namedNathan whom I would soon know as uncle. I met Uncle Nathan at the corner store called "ANS" right by the taco place. He walked by and asked if I was okay. I responded "Yes, I was just praying". Hours later, He returned to the store for a pack of cigarettes. He spoke again but this time to warn me "You might want to move to the other side of the store when it gets dark. It gets dangerous over here at night" He said. Then, He was gone again. After I had moved to the other side, He returned and said "Hey". Just then, It began to rain. So, I signaled for him to get in. He thanked me and then said "I got all the way to the house and right before I went up the steps I heard a whisper said Go back and get her".  All I could think was "wow"! At first, Uncle Nathan was super quiet and shy but then as He got to know me; He began to share many stories of his past with me and even taught me how to get around town. He also told me that He'd once wanted to write a book about his life. I was thankful that He'd opened his home to me but Ahayah revealed to me that soon this too would be called temporary. I quickly learned that Uncle Nathan was dealing with many of his own spiritual wars. Everyone has a past but some struggle a little harder to overcome theirs. UncleNathan had been traumatized by his past and was having a hard time learning to trust again. Sometimes his advice was overbearing but I'm sure he meant well. He was kind but there were times where a dark manipulative spirit would enter. All in all it was a blessing to be taken in by someone that wasn't trying to hurt me and seemingly sincere. I just had to remember that my trust was to be placed in YaShaya and not in man.

On my third night staying at Uncle Nathan' house we had an altercation due to an invasion of my privacy. He'd been drinking and that could be the reason his judgment was clouded. Still he had no excuse for what he did and how he behaved afterwards. There was a thick tension through the night and I was uncomfortable about going back to sleep. Around 1am I packed up my things and went to sleep in my car but down the street in front of S.O.G's home. Uncle Nathan was so mean to the puppy he'd given me so I took Sabbakey with me. Stylez was still staying with S.O.G so he met me outside and stayed with me until I grew sleepy. Then, right as I began to fall asleep a heavy rain began to pour down. It's amazing how Ahayah has a way of providing us with peace in the midst of a storm. I awoke a few times and found that S.O.G had been awake and spotted me outside. I remember thinking "What had I done to make this man so angry and bent on hurting me"?

Regardless of the reason I feared not. When I arose I found that Stylez had been led to believe that I'd left and came back for no reason at all. Why was my fiancé told that I left in the middle of the night and returned. Where would I have gone? Why would I lie? I couldn't worry myself with those who were allowing the enemy to use them in his schemes.

When the sun came up I left and went to the store. Then, I decided to pull up on Uncle Nathan to try and reconcile the issue. The first attempt was unsuccessful and I left Sabbakey with him so that he could eat and poop. I returned to where I'd been parked on the first day that I'd encountered Uncle Nathan. While sitting there I received a call from my spiritual mother Mel. A woman which I looked up to because of her strong faith and overcoming obstacles in life. Her daughter had been my best friend for several years even down to the title of my big sister. Mama Mel and I would talk on the phone for hours about The Most High and the plans that He'd revealed to us. I loved our talks and they were so easy to get lost in. I thought it was strange how she always knew when to call. Mama Mel had blessed me with a few dollars to get food and cigarettes. So, that's where I headed.

On the way to pick up Stylez, I got another call. S.O.G had put Stylez out. I became angry because I knew it was out of spite towards me. However, I reassured my man that Ahayah was still in control and that He always has a plan. We had to realize it and have faith that we were covered no matter what we experienced. I received another call. This time it was Uncle Nathan. He was calling to tell me that Sabbakey was looking for me. I laughed when he'd told me that Sabbakey had followed my scent back to the store and Uncle Nathan had to chase him all the way to the store parking lot. That story made my day . We spoke about Sabbakey for a few more moments and then Uncle Nathan apologized sincerely. I forgave him and apologized as well. Then, I told him what happened with Stylez and S.O.G. He offered us both a place to park and his facilities to use. I considered just that to be a blessing. Understanding that a man usually doesn't want to help a man because they feel a man should be being a man; we happily accepted the offer. We'd be safe and could keep ourselves clean.

After the first night, something amazing happened. We'd been invited into Uncle Nathan' home to stay until we could get on our feet. Uncle Nathan harbored so much hurt and anger from past experiences. I just wanted to show that we were appreciative and that we considered him family too. Once again, I was in awe of the blessings that The Most High had bestowed upon us. We had both been blessed with jobs, a roof over our heads, food, and fellowship. We were approved for our food stamps and were awaiting the card through the mail. Since the card was going to S.O.G's address we would have to endure just a little while longer. Nevertheless, we remained in strong faith and deep prayer while waiting. I ended up having to complete an address change form. I visited the post office and confided in a supervisor whom I appealed to. He agreed to help me by letting our mail be held for pickup each week. Praise Ahayah for he was always working in mysterious ways on our behalf. I felt accomplished because I knew that I could do all things through Christ YaShaya.

A Few days later, after taking Stylez to work; I pulled back up to the house where I found Uncle Nathan on the front porch struggling with his radio. I thought to myself "Who even uses radios anymore?" I told him to come with me because I had a surprise for him. I took him with me back to Rose's. This was the same store he'd shown me only a few days before. I could never forget the expression on his face which showed so much gratitude. I'd bought him, Stylez, and myself each bluetooth speakers. Bye-bye Mr. Static radio! I also showed him how to use it. He was always sitting on that porch wrestling with the radio to get a clear gospel station. Now he would just find the music he wanted to hear and press play on his phone. That speaker was a game changer and he could still program the radio stations on it. I felt that the spirit had placed it on my heart to do it, so I did. As the days went by, I would get up and take my Stylez to work and then set out to accomplish each task on my todo list. I had to remember the words of my spiritual mother Mel. "Just keep moving forward with faith, Daughter." So everyday I got up and went to the post office but each day there was nothing yet.

    Something powerful was happening and I could feel it. I was being strengthened and prepared. Suddenly, one day while scrolling on IG I came across a promoter from Atlanta, reached out, and resulted in being invited to perform. I believed that this was arranged by Ahayah so I began to plead with each of my family members for funding to make this 3 hr drive. Stylez also took a leap of faith with me and requested Thursday off so we could prepare and arrive on time.

## Chapter 12

## No Weapon Formed

    We made it to Atlanta 3 hours early. We stopped at a beauty supply store so that I could replace my nose ring. While in line I ended up doing a little last minute promoting. I went back out to the car where Stylez was waiting. He ended up parking on the other side of the parking lot by a burger king. We still had a couple of hours to kill so Stylez just used the time to network and promote both of our music. He's always been so good at networking and drawing people. So that day he managed to grab the attention of a few strangers in the parking lot drawing them in by playing our music out loud. They loved it and told us we had something special. We'd definitely gained a few new supporters in Atlanta. Shortly after, we witnessed a couple fighting in that same parking lot. It caught my attention and I wished I could help them in some way. The concern must have been obvious on my face because Stylez interrupted my thoughts saying "Mind your own baby".
    I felt blessed to have a man that cared enough to lead me away from drama, so I left it alone. We headed to the club and parked across the street at around nine pm. We were finally there and the mission was almost complete. We hit a few more snags before actually getting inside, but nothing that faith in YaShaya couldn't rearrange. We were the only ones in our VIP section and that was fine with us. I didn't need a bottle and we'd spent all the money we gathered on gas and wardrobe, so we didn't have any cigarettes either. None of that mattered

at the time. This was the night that I would show Atlanta what they were missing and I did. I must've rocked the show pretty good because afterward I was approached by a different ATL promoter named Caprice. We hit it off instantly and I wondered if that was the plan all along. All I know is that Ahayah works in mysterious ways.

The mission was completed! Now it was time for us to get back to Albany. We'd spent all of our money getting there so we would have to, as usual, trust Ahayah, to get us there, and He did. I ended up falling asleep most of the ride home, but Stylez asked me to wake up to help him stay awake, so I did. I love this man. We always find ourselves reminiscing and talking about how thankful we are that Ahayah gave us to each other. We both believed that we were predestined and ordained for one another. There were many positive aspects of our relationship but one in particular is that no matter what we experienced, The Most High always reminded us that He was with us through it all. We made it home around 5 am and immediately went to bed. We had to get right back up so Stylez could get to work by 10 am.

Things would soon take a weird turn and The Most High had even warned me a few times before it happened so that when the time came, we knew not to worry. Another fruit of the spirit is discernment and it was upon me strongly lately. Despite Uncle Nathan having offered to empty his second bedroom for us to stay; Ahayah had already shown me the reservations with our names written for a place we'd soon call home by the end of May. We'll eventually get to that but, right now let's get into the weird series of events that led to our next victory. On the Sunday before, Uncle Nathan was supposed to close out my Zoom sermon in benediction. Instead, he began to act uneasy and bothered moments before I started the zoom, then He wound up leaving until the zoom was over. I wondered why and what was really going on. I had an idea, but no way to prove it. So, I didn't touch on it until three or four days later. I had become a lifelong student. So, there are many things which I have yet to learn from my teacher YaShaya. At that time, I hadn't yet known that a woman should not become a preacher unless she is under the leadership of a man and appointed. I know this will bring a lot of controversy but It is written and true. Think I am lying? Read it for yourself 1 Timothy 2:12.

That's when things began to escalate almost at the speed of light. There was a familiar spirit warring against me through Nathan. Could this have been the same spirit which dwelled in S.O.G? Why Uncle Nathan? Why S.O.G? Were they just randomly chosen vessels or had they harbored enough sinful energy to where this nephilim didn't need an invite. Anyhow, this time it wasn't alone. I could see in Nathan's eyes and was reminded again of his actions from the night before. When Saturday came, it was time for the final stand off between Stylez, Nathan, and I. I was so proud of the way that my man was led by the Rawach to defend and protect me. No violence was used, only words and wisdom. Regardless, We have to remember that the battle was not even truly ours. I prayed and rebuked the spirits which temporarily dwelled within Nathan's body, but I knew that this stay had made it's final call. So, we quickly grabbed our things and left. The Most High told us to go and we did. Although it saddened me to lose Uncle Nathan it was painfully obvious that these events had to happen. We couldn't get comfortable until this second mission was complete. We had to be led away from hindrances and I understood how that would have become one if we hadn't left. Strange that Stylez had gotten his first paycheck that very same day. Uncle Nathan never set a price nor required a payment arrangement for us staying there. We considered that with all of the rides without gas, the random gifts, cleaning, cooking, taking care of Sabbakey, and buying his requested six packs daily, that he would be appreciative to receive forty bucks and a six pack of beer. He wanted more, but didn't know how to express that.

I recall seeing the blue jay playing with a baby cardinal in the yard the day before. Protection, is what it exhibited to me. That resonated so deeply at the moment. Honestly the departure wasn't as bad as it could have been, so We sent praises up to The Most High, Ahayah, for his wisdom and guidance once again. Then, we headed over to Ray's. He was one of Stylez' first Albany haircut clients and soon became a close friend of ours. We chilled there for a few hours which allowed me to get caught up on my writing and daily biblical studies. Although We knew we couldn't stay, that moment was peaceful. More grapes in the wilderness! When It was time for us to leave we had nowhere in particular to go. So, We parked at the familiar truck stop down the road. We were both tired and sleepy. Stylez didn't want us to go back to sleeping in the car and by the mercy and grace of Ahayah we had just enough to get a room for a week. We went forth in search of shelter. I also called around town but keep in mind it was about 1 am. We'd finally found a place. It wasn't far from Stylez' job so we would conserve gas. It wasn't the Hilton but it was clean, had a bed, and a shower. Perfect! Ahayah had kept us under His grace once more and given us rest. Little did we know, we were just a few steps closer to our promised home and many more blessings.

## Chapter 13

## The Power of Fasting

During the first 3 days of our hotel stay, I began to fast and on the last day of that fast a blessing was released. Our food stamp card had finally come. Praise Ahayah! I was fasting for a breakthrough and one came. The whole week we searched for a home and we were denied a few times but that small discouragement couldn't break our faith. We were reprogrammed to operate completely off of faith and only depend on YaShaya for everything we'd receive. We were being tested although we fought a few times, pressed by frustration; each time we were able to quickly make up and remind one another of the love that Ahayah has blessed us to have. Saturday came faster than we thought it would. That marked our last day in the one-week stay at the 8 Inn of Albany.

We packed up once we were asked to pay for another night or leave. Our exit was graceful and we used this time to go and visit the familiar water place. We had stopped and gotten food for a spontaneous lunch date. It was beautiful and pleasant. While there we Face-timed Stylez' daughter Lyana. It was so amazing because a few weeks before Stylez had mentioned a lunch at the park and said nothing more since then. When we left we went to a less crowded but even more beautiful water place. This time we were greeted by songbirds. They urged me to continue my songs of praise strategically. Each time that I would stop singing they got further away but while I sang they'd draw closer. Stylez realized what they were doing and asked me to sing louder so that I could see. They began to join in as if we were a choir. That's so powerful!

What happened next was miraculous. We'd come to be alone with The Most High and He'd accepted our invite. We began to notice the clouds forming words and numbers, but something truly intended for our eyes appeared in the sky. Bayath was written in the clouds. Only The Most High would know that I could recognize the second Hebrew letter which means "House of" or "House". Looking back, when we first arrived at the second water place we'd encountered a man named Willie. Stylez was led to ask him about rental availability and he gave us a number to his landlord. Stylez used one of my old notebooks to write it down and while calling and waiting for an answer He'd began blindly drawing a very descriptive picture of a man. This picture was so detailed and when I asked about it he was clueless. He'd drawn a man with a bald thinning and long straight hair. The man also had a narrow pointed nose. It was someone I'd never seen yet could never forget.

We ended up getting a call from Troy and being invited to his son's birthday gathering. We stopped and got him a small gift, gas and then finally arrived back at Troy's house. To our surprise the house was empty and this brought on a little confusion but soon we were able to reach him and receive directions to his aunt's house. She didn't live very far from him.

Upon our arrival, Stylez unknowingly revealed that He'd actually been there before. I wasn't bothered by the fact that he had been. I was bothered that He hid it or never mentioned it. We talk about everything so what would make him omit the truth of one of his visits with Troy. I knew this was the enemy trying to anger me and I refused to let him attack my mind. I completed the home application that I was filling out and then got out to introduce myself. Later during the party, a small window of opportunity presented itself. Once again it was time to usher in the Rawach. A conversation regarding my book arose. Obviously I was prepared to give YaShaya the floor.

Vanessa is Troy's sister and Lizzie Pearl is his aunt. I remembered Ahayah showing me the name Elizabeth earlier that week. I began to speak about what was given unto me concerning their names and each one's meaning. I sat and conversed with Auntie Liz a while longer and then Vanessa joined us again. In such a short time we reached a deep level of Aunt Lisa's suffering. She even began to pour out the hurt and pain to me. She'd buried it under a well of alcohol and now it was time to release it. All of it!

This woman was nowhere near crazy as others had come to believe. She was called to be set apart and tormented by evil for that very reason. She felt heavy with this load and didn't understand it herself. I assured her that the victory was already won through Christ. Her ring soon caught my attention. It was beautiful and sapphire blue. It turned out to be the color of her birthstone. She told me the story of how she came to possess it and that too was beautiful. Before leaving she'd asked me to pray for her and I did as I promised.

Vanessa was still there for a few moments after Aunt Lisa left. We both agreed that we would meet again and talk more. I knew from her questions that soon her quest for the truth would begin. I remember feeling blessed and understanding that it is an honor to be used by The Most High. We stayed a little longer than everyone else. Eventually, Troy's aunt named Tina beckoned for me to come speak with her in the kitchen. She wanted to show me the beautiful head wraps that she makes. They were amazingly hand-knitted and sewn. She also has face masks but I felt no need for them. We began to talk and dig deeper. She even gifted me a head wrap of my own to keep. It was so pretty and felt as if it were majestic. Mine was orange, gold, black and white. It reminded me of golden nuggets and orange flowers. I was so appreciative and soon It'd be time to reciprocate. A gift of knowledge and wisdom which was bestowed upon me and now unto her. She insisted that I eat and after resisting a few times I gave in. We sat there in the kitchen and talked for hours about everything Ahayah has shown me. We also talked about all that He has done for her and her family. His wonders and miracles keep me in awe. Our conversations required us both to dig deep into past experiences. This soon brought us to the revelation that we were there by design. If you zakar (which is again Hebrew for recall or remember) "there are no coincidences". It was starting to get late so we said our "see ya laters" and headed out.

    Initially, we planned to go back and park by the 8 Inn but after Stylez noticed a strange man waving different shaped and sized weapons in the air. He awoke me and we decided it was best to relocate. Shortly after driving out of the parking lot, I fell back asleep and was rudely awakened by a sharp turn. Stylez had forgotten the way back to the truck stop and grown tired of driving. So we ended up resting wherever we would park. Have you ever been so sleepy that you couldn't fight it and then the next thing you know you're wishing you could get back to sleep but can't? Well, that's what happened to me that night. Almost as soon as Stylez parked in these abandoned apartments, I was stuck in woke mode. I heard every insect crawling, animal prowling, and the water flowing from a nearby pond. How was I supposed to get back to sleep now? Meanwhile, Stylez was exiting the car for a potty break. Maybe it wasn't meant for us to go back to sleep right away.

## Chapter 14

## The Bullfrog's Call

Soon Stylez returned to the car claiming to have heard a strange loud noise. Initially, I hadn't heard it but once He'd brought it to my attention we both heard it. It was weird and unlike any animal sound, either of us had ever witnessed. We began to hear it more frequently and eventually we were overcome by curiosity. I googled multiple animal sounds and listened to each of them until we found it. It was a bullfrog! Of all the animals we suspected, none of them were anywhere near close to a bull frog. It was actually quite funny. It was amazing! We'd grown annoyed with one another and were bickering every few minutes until the bull frog discovery. We laughed so hard and began acting silly, making jokes about the discovery. We instantly forgot why we were even bickering in the first place.

The next day we were invited to visit Troy and his family out in the country. It was a great day and a perfect opportunity to spread the Word. When we first touched down we mingled with Vanessa and Aunt Tish for a minute. Stylez ended up giving Troy's uncle a free haircut for his birthday. He was so appreciative. We hadn't even known it was his birthday until moments before the haircut was offered. We knew he was appreciative because he wouldn't stop talking to Stylez about his new fade. Next we headed down the street where the family was gathered at the park. I really don't like bugs so I decided to stay in the car listening to music and catching up on writing.

Before leaving the city we'd stopped and grabbed some snacks and I was kind of hungry so I pulled them out. It was almost like clock work. The kids came from nowhere. You would think they had a supernatural sense of smell the way that they swarmed the car with their hands out. I missed my kids and I have always loved children so of course I gave in.

One of them was an 11 year old boy named Shon. Even after the snacks were gone he kept popping up and talking my ear off. It was okay, he was a sweet young man. The rest of them would make their way back around every thirty minutes or so. While the kiddos were occupying my time with a wide range of questions, Stylez had it placed upon his heart to offer some more haircuts. He ended up making about $25. Praise Ahayah for He'd once again provided for us. We enjoyed ourselves and were welcomed by everyone with open arms. I would definitely say we gained more than money that day. Eventually we made our way over to another one of Troy's aunts. Her name is Auntie Anne. Stylez and I were playing our music for the kids out front when She sent a few of Troy's kinfolk to come get me. She wanted me to properly introduce myself and so I did. We had a beautiful conversation about Ahayah's name which is found in Exodus 3:10-15. We also went into the history of the Hebrews and how the bible was originally written in our language. I felt so accomplished because my soul mission had become to encourage and uplift others with the truth of YaShaya and his word. Mission complete! Before heading back to the city we made one final stop. I can't remember his name but it was Troy's brother. He just wanted to see his nephew before we left.

When we were heading out Troy seemed super irritated. This was interesting because I'd never seen him upset before. We started out following behind Troy but I think his anger had taken over and somewhere along the line he'd forgotten we were there. One minute he was right in front of us and then the next he was gone. His car was nowhere in sight. We ended up using the gps to get back to Albany. Once we'd made it everything began to look familiar again. We were starting to learn our way around the city but still had a lot more to learn. We arrived at the same abandoned apartments from before and were immediately greeted by the bullfrog. We were now used to the strange sound so sleep wouldn't be an issue. Also, we'd stopped for bathroom breaks before getting there so we were good for the night. I guess you could say we were better prepared due to our prior learning experience. Each experience brought us closer to the point at which Ahayah intended us to be. Actually, each experience brought us closer to Ahayah and increased our faith in YaShaya. The next day we were blessed to have a hotel room. We were so appreciative and grateful for even just one night of rest in an actual bed again that we didn't mind the possibility that we'd be back in the car the next night. We'd learned to count every blessing even the small ones because they are all extended by grace. We were blessed again after that hotel stay with another. The Most High was showering us in his favor.That night I was encouraged to begin a five day fast. So that is exactly what I did. When we arose we went house hunting once more and wound up at a new water place. A moment of peace which I would usually call more grapes in the wilderness.

  We found ourselves in awe of another one of Ahayah's beautiful creations. While there I began to praise Him in the form of a song. I wasn't singing very loudly until the songbirds came and joined in again. After all, I had many reasons to sing. Stylez encouraged my singing and motioned for me to do it louder. "Sing unto the lord of Israel." A voice in my head whispered. All praises go to none other. All I could think of was David the faithful servant after Ahayah's own heart. More birds came and joined over the few hours we were there. It was as miraculous as any other time, yet more powerful. I knew that all of our prayers were being heard and answered. Afterward, we resumed our house hunt.

I started to pray quietly while Stylez was driving. We had no specific destination nor direction. Next something amazing happened. The Holy Spirit began to whisper coordinates in my ear: Go left, go right and she even said keep going he's almost there. My initial question was "Who?" I suddenly understood that this was literal and not figurative. I somehow ended up trading places with Stylez and taking over the wheel. That's when we realized we were blocking someone we'd just passed from re-entering his driveway. I immediately apologized and attempted to move out of his way but for some reason the man was trying to flag us down. Ahayah was stirring up something in the pot of Heaven. A few mysteries were about to be revealed right before our eyes. Timing, patience, and faith are all key components to remember along this type of quest.

One minute we were driving around the city aimlessly and the next we were parked in front of a location we'd soon grow to love. We had yet to even break the ice of understanding what The Most High was doing.

## Chapter 15

## Picture This

    Eventually, the man approached the car and introduced himself. His name was Henry. He had two beautiful puppies with him as well. I suppose they were saying hello to us only in a dog's language. Mr. Henry was so welcoming and helpful. He even gave us 2 rental property leads and a brief yet detailed history on each of them. He told us about the best areas to live in and the worst. He even gave us the number to call his landlord, Mr. Sounds. We later called him but at that specific moment, Henry asked us to back up the car until he said stop. Next, He told us to look to the left and there it was. There was no for rent sign but apparently, we were looking at a two-story townhome recently vacated and now for rent. He told us that it was once inhabited by a young girl with a child until one day a few weeks back she just packed up most of her things and left. How convenient we both thought.

    After speaking with Mr. Henry, we understood that The Most High had prepared a place for us and that all of these events were arranged in advance. We called Mr. Sounds as soon as we left and made reference to our encounter with Mr. Henry. We later found that Mr. Henry was not only a tenant to Mr. Sounds but also his personal property maintenance man. It's important to remember that The Most High can and will use anyone He pleases. Moving forward, we ended up setting a date and time to view the house. We loved it! There were no designer tiles nor see-through showers like the homes we'd viewed the past few weeks but it was spacious, clean, had two bathrooms, a nice kitchen, office space, and a second bedroom for the return of my kids. It wasn't perfect but it was perfect for us. This would be a huge blessing and a foundation to build our new lives upon. A week later we were approved but had no money to move in. YaShaya kept finding ways to assure me that this would all work out. One thing that was obvious is that we were truly being brought out of this stage in our lives.

No more homelessness, bouncing around from house to house, and staying with others in the form of worn-out visitors. We signed our lease on the following Thursday on May 27, 2021. This was a big accomplishment and all of the praise and honor goes to The Most High. He'd empowered us, caused us to prevail in the hardest times, and shown his light upon us in the darkest moments. Even the day before we signed our lease, we'd hit a snag. We drove around all day looking for a car loan office that would work with out-of-state loanees. We must have driven out all of our gas during the search because before we knew it, the gas tank was under the E line. Neither of us said anything out loud but YaShaya heard our silent prayers.

We were in the parking lot of Titlemax when a car backed up quickly into us. The impact wasn't very hard but it did cause a small scratch. The owner was an elderly man who at the time we didn't know was struggling with an illness and medical bills. That was something that YaShaya was about to unveil to us. The man was afraid that we'd call the police but Stylez kept him calm and was led by the Holy Spirit to negotiate a mutually beneficial agreement. The man was appreciative and happily gave us one hundred dollars. Now we had the money for a full tank of gas and also a hotel room for the night. Right after the incident, I proceeded inside to speak with a loan agent. She'd seen the incident on the store camera. She asked if everyone was okay and I assured her that no one was hurt. She then went on to tell me that the man was ill and had been a faithful loanee for quite a while, wrestling with the payments of medical bills and medications. I felt the Holy Spirit warm my heart in sympathy. I then understood and we began the loan info process, only to conclude with negative results once again. Before going to get the hotel room we came to one last office which was called Loan Max. Finally, we had found a place that would work with us. We needed fourteen hundred dollars but we were only approved for one thousand. Regardless this was a start! We were blessed to be able to get that so there was no need to complain. We prayed and had faith that The Most High would finish what He'd started and that's exactly what He did.

The next morning it was time to meet with the landlord for the official signing and to get the keys. We were excited and practiced good faith in being optimistic. We arrived at our new home early and began to make a few phone calls to see if we could borrow the other four hundred from members of either of our families. My mom was willing to send us what she could and so was my uncle but we'd still be a couple hundred short. We needed another miracle!

Sometimes a miracle doesn't have to be physically giving. In my experience, I have found that wisdom itself is a miracle and at that moment it was granted to me. While on the phone with my mom and uncle Matthew, an idea was given to each of us but only spoken out of my uncle's mouth. It was crazy enough to work. I would call the landlord before he arrived and explain that we had a certain amount and ask if we could arrange payments in addition to the first three months of rent. He hesitated initially but just as I began to silently pray again Mr. Sounds interrupted and said "Let me discuss this idea with my wife and I will call you guys right back."

Needless to say, she did approve and they agreed to work with us. Mr. Sounds congratulated us on our new home once he'd given us the keys and then he pulled Stylez aside and had a man-to-man talk with him. He admired the fact that we operated as husband and wife should. Stylez handed him the payments, Led the conversations, and brought order to our relationship as far as Mr. Sounds could see and that is how it should've been although it truly wasn't. We won't go into that right now, just understand that once again the victory was ours through faith in Christ and perseverance. We offered praises to Ahayah. This mountain that once stood tall before us in the form of an obstacle was now broken and shattered into pieces of earth. Not only was it moved but through Christ, it was dismantled in our favor. Although the electricity was not on yet we still decided that we would sleep in our home the same night. There was a sofa still inside left by the girl who'd lived there right before us and also I went ahead and prayed for purification over every doorway, wall, closet, mirror, and window.

Our Heavenly Father had truly been gracious unto us and had hedged us under his protection from harm. It was later revealed that the man from the picture that Stylez had drawn while at the water place, was Mr. Henry. During the first few months, He and his brother lived directly across the street from us. He was still very helpful even after helping us find our house. When he moved, it took us a minute to realize he had because just the act of bringing him up in conversation led to him mysteriously appearing. Isn't that interesting?! Anyways, I'm not saying life is going to be perfect from now on or anything like that but, I am saying that I've learned from our past and recent experiences to put all of my trust in YaShaya. I now understand that we live in a pagan world and must rely on Ahayah's spirit to navigate through each obstacle. Despite all of the enemy's attacks, I remain in strong faith. Even though there are times that are more trying than others, I continue to trust that The Most High has a plan for us. Us being all of those who have been blessed with eyes to see, ears to hear, and a tongue to praise The Almighty Ahayah. Those who are called out of the darkness and into the light. I am speaking to those who have and will be granted the wisdom to understand that the only way out is through. This quest has taught deeper meanings of many things and revealed truths of which were hidden in dark caves; buried as ruins.

## Chapter 16

# As In the Days of Noah

You know that old saying "What doesn't kill you makes you stronger?" That would be perfectly applied to this story. For instance, everything that the enemy uses to execute an attack on our lives, faith, hearts, and mind become the very things that YaShaya uses to strengthen and build us up. Ultimately, it is for the glory of Ahayah. I used to be so afraid of being alone and in the dark that I would tolerate unhealthy company. YaShaya showed me that I am never alone and that my soul was more valuable than I'd been tricked into believing. I am no longer afraid of the dark because light has been placed within me. I desire for that same light to shine into all of you and that if you don't already know him, you will seek and find YaShaya after reading this.

Another very important thing to reflect on is that, where this story begins; I hadn't yet known the true name of The Most High. Honestly, after being hit by that car in 2019; I was tricked by the enemy into worshiping Yahweh who is also known as the Egyptian moon god, Jupiter to the Romans, Zeus to the Greek and many other names that I am sure you've heard in history. There were many traps and snares set before me on this quest. Allow me to elaborate. It all started with prayer which led to meditation. The enemy knew that I was a babe in seeking the truth and willing to do anything to show my appreciation to YaShaya for keeping me from death. I didn't understand the spiritual aspect of everything yet. All I knew was that Christ meditated in the bible and that I aspired to be like Christ. I didn't quite comprehend that the meditation Christ practiced was actually meditating on the word of Ahayah in prayer. After all He did come to fulfill the law and prophecies given to Moses and the prophets who came after. This is according to Matthew 5:17-19. Actually, this new-age meditation isn't really "new" at all.

In fact, it is the very same practice that the biblical heathen and gentiles used to communicate with the fallen angels whom they exalted as gods. Thus, the commandment stating "Thou shalt not serve any gods besides me". Unknowingly, at that time this is exactly what I'd fallen into. Strange things began to happen. I began seeking the wrong information out of confusion. Satan thought he'd won my soul. I became so passionate about meditating, buying crystals, finding ancient literature, and learning the ways of my ancestors. I even taught others these false doctrines. The Most High had a plan to bring it all together even when It appeared I was lost to Lucifer or Samael's lies forever. Doors were opening in all the wrong locations for me. I soon realized there were people I've known for almost fifteen years doing these same practices and worships. How could I have never known? It was as if I had just been initiated into a dark, secret satanic cult. The music I wrote began to focus more on sex, drugs, and power. It had become even more accepted than before. Why not? After all, I was being used by the fallen ones and their nephilim children to influence and confuse. Drugs were easier than ever to find and with the dark arts as my influence tool; Seduction, finesse, and trickery all became well-developed skills.

Men whom I never imagined approaching were becoming like putty in my hands. I was beginning not to care for anyone except for my best friend and the angels we were worshiping. I began dating Stylez around this time almost a year later. Unlike the others I'd toyed and quickly grown bored with; He didn't do drugs other than smoking green and he was a challenge to the demonic spirits that counseled me at that time. I couldn't control nor finesse him and eventually, he was used by YaShaya to pull me away from everything evil in my life. Even when I met him he saw beyond my mask. He wasn't perfect nor without sin but he began unknowingly watering the seed I mentioned earlier. He didn't preach to me or anything but he was knowledgeable of the word and would often quote scriptures which would spark small bolts of conviction in me. I was in deep with this evil deception I'd stumbled into. I wouldn't go anywhere without my crystals, I believed they were protecting me, and I'd made a pact of witchcraft with my two best friends. I understand now that these were soul ties being created.

Something happened when Trey died. I started to question this so-called spirituality. I wanted to know more. The Most High led me to the exact answers.

These practices were in the bible! As many times as I have read this bible I never understood what I was reading as clearly as it had become right then. Many of you might know this as a familiar moment of epiphany. The Hebrews were punished for doing those very things. No wonder people would always lead with "It's the way of our ancestors". It was the way of our ancestors. By doing so, they were being deliberately disobedient of the laws given to Moses by The Most High. Even before the deliverance of our people from the bondage of Egypt, The Most High commanded us not to do these things but after Eve's sin Satan devised a plan. It was he and the fallen ones who'd given humans the practices of corrupting natural herbs, splicing DNA, sorcery, spells, and even knowledge of things we should have never known. This is all according to The Book of Enoch and supported by many scriptures in the 1611 King James Bible. Almost as soon as Yashaya had awakened me to some of the truth, this quest began. Eventually , I was led to find my church GOCC and more watering of the seed occurred.

I'd always questioned how Christ's name was Jesus when the fact still stood that the letter "J" wasn't even invented until later in the 15th century. Slowly, my eyes were bucking open and I was realizing all of the lies which the Synagogue of Satan had been feeding us for thousands of years. Finally, I was blessed with confirmation for the true names of Ahayah and YaShaya once we were settled into the new home. I'd witnessed the Elders of GOCC breaking down and translating Exodus 3 in its original Hebrew writings. In Exodus 3:13, Moses specifically asks The Most High "When the children of Israel ask what is his name, what shall I say unto them"? Then in Exodus 3:14 The Most High answers and says "I AM THAT I AM". In Masoretic Hebrew(Hebrew with vowels) His name would be "Ehyeh Asher Ehyeh" but during the time of Exodus that form of Hebrew hadn't come along yet. So, His name is "Ahayah Ashar Ahayah". To truly understand what has been revealed to myself and many others, You must forget the lies and cover ups that you once thought were the truth. Once Ahayah's true name had been taught to me, I craved more wisdom. This wisdom would only come from The Holy Spirit and those who were sent forth to teach it.

A few weeks later Christ's true name was revealed to me along with many other hidden truths. Once I began working at my new job, I became capable of affording to enroll in the Hebrew and Bible Academy through GOCC. I became more fluent in the language of Hebrew and then possessed a new tool for the continuation of this quest. I pray that just by reading this, that your faith strengthens and increases. I wanted you all to not only know this story but to highlight the key factor as the power of Christ so that you may also begin to seek and trust in him to aid in your quest. Remember that faith is light and light is truth. If you have faith in Christ anything is possible. No, I didn't become a super rich tv star, but I learned the truth about who I am, who Christ is, and what my true purpose was always meant to be. By having the truth, I am equipped for anything thrown my way

## Chapter 17

# Positioned

We must not forget that everything has its season. Nothing is ever done in vain, even if it appears that way . If you think you have seen all there is to be seen, then you can not see all there is to be seen. We all have read that The Most High never gives us more than we can bare. I truly believe that! We often receive a message or assignment and automatically according to our human nature, assume that it means what we think it means. I am also guilty of this. So let's take a moment to be reminded that we cannot lean on our own understanding and reason but seek truth and revelation while trusting Christ to lead us in every way possible. Yes, I know that is easier said than done but it can be done. Let's hold on to that while we move forward.

We made our 1 year engagement official during an interesting trip to Texas. Although I was excited that we'd finally set a date to be married; I strongly felt Stylez' hesitation. I'd hoped he'd express what he was worried about or why he was hesitant. It got worse though. He literally waited until the day before our appointment to go get our marriage license, to tell me he didn't want to get married. I was distraught over the way he'd done it. I explained to him how we couldn't be pleasing in Ahayah's eyes if we continued to live this willingly sinful life. I told him how bad it hurt but I felt that we could no longer be together. I tried so hard to be gentle at the same time my heart felt like it exploded into pieces. I had come to understand that there were specific things required of not only me but anyone who makes the decision to leave behind everything and follow Christ YaShaya. I had to think of you. Yes, YOU! You and anyone else who would one day read this book in hopes of being inspired. I am surely no teacher as 1 Timothy 2:12 confirms but, I do believe that we often learn from watching others. I went through an entire speech with supportive scriptures and all. Stylez grew angry, slamming the door, and yelling "never call me again"! That break up lasted for almost two weeks. If this was a test, I definitely failed. We returned home to Georgia unmarried and still living under this specific sin of fornication. I would say that we returned to life as we had come to know it but I'd be lying. I was beginning to fear the punishment of living in willful sin. We started to have arguments regarding our sexual life, bills, him not being employed anymore, and many small insignificant issues as well. The pressures of disorder were eating at me.

While in Texas, I began and completed the 4 week baptism course. The Bishop agreed that I could be baptized in Georgia since I had to return home to start a new job. We were home for about two weeks before our electricity was disconnected due to a large bill amount. We were blessed once again to be able to get a hotel room until we could gather the funds to get it back on. Remember there are no coincidences so would you believe me if I told you that while in the hotel room with Stylez and my daughter; I was the only one to contract an illness. Eventually, I was able to borrow the money from my cousin Nicci; who by the way was becoming curious regarding The Truth. All praises! We returned home and the electricity was reconnected. I remained sick throughout the next three months, but that didn't stop me from getting baptized on April 17,2022 at 12:08 pm. I knew that being baptized would stir up some spirits around me but I never knew what exactly to expect.

Stylez had been there for me during my baptism. It was such a beautiful experience; especially considering the fact that I am not a big fan of water. One moment I felt afraid and then the next I wasn't worried at all. I came up out of the water feeling like I had just claimed a major victory. I felt like this was the beginning of a new chapter in my life; A prerequisite for entry into the kingdom. Over the next few weeks I had many encounters that would require the wisdom that could only be given by The Holy Spirit. What a blessing for me, I had been given and received exactly that. It started to seem that the closer I got to Christ, the more Stylez and I fought. Something in me could no longer willingly submit to sinful behaviors. I could no longer condone his habits and lifestyle. Once again It was time to make a decision. I wasn't being condescending but, I had to choose to please man or Ahayah. I had waited long enough and I had stalled for as long as I could but I knew what my instructions were. I understood the assignment. I just hated the idea of what the right choice would mean for Stylez and my relationship. I prayed and prayed but my instructions stayed the same.

  I even sometimes wondered if there was a work around but we all know that we can't pull the wool over The Most High Ahayah's eyes. Once again, I felt my heart breaking into pieces but this had to be done. If I knew nothing else, I knew that I had to be obedient. So I began to pray to find out when to do this, how to do it, and for The Holy Rawach to give me the words to speak while doing it. Eventually, it was done and after we had this emotionally disturbing conversation I knew that Christ had stood beside me the entire time. I knew that I had angered many of the spirits operating within Stylez but I wasn't afraid. I bought his plane ticket a week in advance. That last week was the most bipolar week in the history of weeks. One day we were hugged up watching movies with Noni as a family, like we weren't in the middle of a life changing process and then the next Stylez was angry and drunk while cursing, being disrespectful, and shouting idle time. There was a day of drunkenness and crying on which I almost broke and gave in.

The Thursday before he left a situation arose. He was extremely drunk that night and grew angry again. This time it was random disrespectful remarks towards The Most High and the elders of GOCC. At the time It angered me and that is probably what he wanted but, It didn't stop there. It resulted in sleep but not before me compromising to keep it all from escalating. I didn't know how to feel anymore. That was the worst night of sleep and finally Friday came. I had gotten to the point where I was so ready to be away from him and at the same time I couldn't imagine my life without him. Despite all of these emotions and the indecisiveness, I proceeded in obedience. I had dealt with so much pain since returning from Texas and keep in mind that I was still terribly ill. The day flew by and it was peaceful considering the events that had taken place all week. I had an extra powerful prayer/praise session that morning and I was ready for the worst. Though it never came.

    The Most High had heard my prayers and had granted me wisdom once more. So when night fell, before anything inappropriate could happen I screamed out "FAMILY MOVIE NIGHT"! Before either of us could move, Noni entered the room with her blanket and stuffed unicorn Destiny. Stylez side eyed me and whispered "You ain't slick" in my ear. That's when I got up and pulled out the air mattress for Noni. I knew that she would fall asleep halfway through the movie and after taking 2 melatonins so would I. I even offered him one and he took it but he was still a little salty about the whole situation. I know many of you are wondering "what is so bad about having sex with him again after all the times I have"? The difference is knowing James 4:17. This scripture specifically addresses that those who know to do good and what is good in the eyes of Ahayah are to do just that and if they do bad when they know to do good then they are in sin. It was as I'd originally written during the time of the unimaginable. Stylez had returned, but this time I would be the one to walk away .

## Chapter 18

# The Greatest Love Story

Now it was beginning to make sense as to why Bee said "Stylez and I would have the greatest love story". This just may be one of the greatest love stories and it wasn't about my love for Stylez nor his love for me. No, It was about My love for Ahayah and what I would be willing to leave behind to follow Christ. I was willing to walk away from everything and everyone that I knew. I understood that no relationship was exempt, so I did what I had to do. We all went to bed and woke up super early the next morning. It was Saturday! The day Stylez would board a plane and take my cough of guilt and disobedience along with him. Now, I know how that may sound some type of way, but it literally happened. Do you remember how I mentioned being sick for three months after returning home? Well the last cough I coughed was that day. In fact, it was at the airport. It was a peaceful parting and I am still human, so of course I cried a lot. I knew I had done the right thing.

    The first week was emotional, but not as emotional as his departure week. Noni and I watched a lot of movies, binged our favorite tv show, worked out, and even did a little shopping. None of these things comforted me. Truthfully, they gave me something to do and occupied my mind. Prior to the breakup, I believed the book was finished. Strange how Ahayah literally shows us when we have unfinished business. I was instructed to keep writing, so here it is. I began to fast and pray outside of my usual morning and evening prayers the way that I did before I was led to my house and I could clearly hear YaShaya saying "We've got you". One week later I received an email from my church stating that we had a new building and that we'd be commencing our Shabbat lessons there on the 18th of June. That message was so perfectly timed. What was Ahayah up to ? Why that date? That date was the date we had agreed to be married on. Now would be a day I will never forget.

I used the gps to see how far the drive would be. It was only 3 hours and 52 minutes. I could do that! With no driver's license, expired tags, and even though I had gotten used to Stylez driving everywhere. It was a new dawn, a new day, and I had faith that I could do anything through Christ. So on the night of the Shabbat I spoke to Ahayah and told him that if the sun was up when I awoke I would not drive to church that weekend but, If the sun hadn't come up yet when I awoke that I would go. I know, I know y'all. I set myself up but not for failure though. Wouldn't you know that I woke up to the sound of a bird in my window chirping louder than any bird I've ever heard. I woke up to see how a bird had gotten in my house and there was nothing there when I opened my eyes. I walked over to the window and searched for the bird and that is when It hit me. It was still dark out there and when I looked at the time it was only 5:18 AM. I silently chuckled because I understood what Abba had done and that no one else could take credit for it. I packed our bags, stopped for french toast sticks, gassed up the Civic, prayed for traveling grace, and hit the road. What obstacles are you facing? What fears have paralyzed you? What is Abba Ahayah whispering to you through The Spirit at this very moment? Look at your life and in the words of Bishop Darak "Does it look like your faith"?

Keep in mind that I did not only write this book to tell my story. I wrote it to reach you. I wrote it to inspire, motivate, ignite, spark, plant and most importantly do the will of my father Ahayah in the name of my savior YaShaya. I also wrote it to warn you of the spiritual dangers and worldly deceptions. I wrote it to help gather and prepare those who have been chosen and don't understand what it means to be chosen. Another fun fact is that the Hebrew word for choose or chose is "Bachaar". Understand that while there are some rewards on earth, don't forget our works are being stored up in Heaven for an even greater reward when Christ returns. 1 Corinthians 2:9 tells us that no eye has seen, no ear hath heard, no mind can even imagine all that The Most High has planned for those which He loves.

The Most High blessed me with a place to live while here on earth as a product of obedience and exhibition of faith in many dark times but, who knows what has been stored up for me in Heaven for these same works. With the guidance of The Holy Spirit I was healed, delivered, transformed, and positioned. YaShaya showed me that he would be with me every step of the way, even when it is too dark to see. During one seven-day isolation my entire life was changed for the better. Yashaya taught me how to search my heart for an ought and how to examine myself by the filtration of the Word. I only desire for you to realize that if He can do all of this for me in only a year, Imagine what miracles await you on your "Quest of Faith in the Darkness."

Made in United States
Orlando, FL
01 March 2024